FOREWORD   2018

God is good. The goodness of God is well-grounded in the Bible and expressed memorably in song, most notably in the upbeat "God is good, all the time." On sunny days, when life unfolds smoothly, the truth that "God is good" is often sung and thought without giving critical thought to the expression. But what happens when life takes a bad turn? What song do believers sing when pain replaces pleasure? What do we say about God when the storm strikes and death draws close?

Joel Royce faced what few do at his age. As a young father of seven, physically strong and fit, and serving God as pastor of a local church, he was diagnosed with a brain tumor. Always serious, Joel's tumor was so very dangerous, and the risks posed by the necessary surgery were so great, that he planned his funeral before undergoing surgery.

It is for our benefit that Joel journaled as he walked through the most difficult days of his life. This book draws upon Joel's journal, but more than that, it reveals lessons learned by a man of faith living in the crucible of suffering. I commend this book to you because it is always valuable to listen to a person who has suffered and been forced to consider what is most important. In the end, and through it all, we see in Joel's testimony that God is not only good, but even more profoundly, that "God is still good." -Randy Adams, Executive Director-Treasurer, Northwest Baptist Convention

INTRODUCTION - PREGAME –

The pregame speech

The inspiration for this book comes from my love for football. The format is patterned after a football game. There is a pregame speech, 4 quarters, halftime speech, postgame speech, challenge flags, timeouts, penalty flags, and some commentary. In the first half, each play is a "Get in the Huddle" entry. After the halftime adjustment, the second half turns to a method of study that will help you grow in your faith walk. The timeouts, challenges, penalties and commentary are entries that cover different topics from apologetics, stories, dealing with grief, and so on.

This book is a labor inspired by my suffering. My life changed forever in the evening of Friday,

February 10th, 2017; I was at the store when suddenly my face went numb. I turned to my bride Leslie and slurred out the words that something was wrong. The neurological symptoms were so bad that I couldn't speak and I couldn't feel my right side. We quickly went to the fire department a couple blocks over and they ruled out a stroke; the initial diagnosis was Bells Palsy. After the ambulance ride to the emergency room, I got wheeled back to get a contrast dye MRI.

The scan revealed a tumor. It was the shape of an egg. 2 cm around the top of the oval/egg shaped tumor, 2.6 cm around the bottom and 3 cm long. Due to the location of the tumor, under the brain surface, the risk of biopsy to me was the same as surgery. Five days later I had brain resection surgery which carried a 5% chance of death, 50% chance of being paralyzed on the right side, 45% chance of having various symptom levels of tingling, numbness, and coordination loss. The goal was minimal brain damage. What would the neurosurgeon find? Would the tumor be embedded in brain tissue? Would there be 'fingers' that dove into other brain matter? Would it be encapsulated?

Before the surgery, I planned my funeral with my good friend and partner in ministry Phil Peters; recorded my last words on video to my wife and children; I wrote letters to each of them; these videos and letters are in google docs to this day. As a matter of fact, I have a growing file in my computer called "The Legacy Folder" which I keep notes, letters, and other things I want my kids to have when I'm gone.

The morning of my surgery I woke up way before the five am buzzer. I woke up afraid. I went into the bathroom and dropped to my knees and asked God to put a song on my heart. I was hungry, thirsty, tired and scared; then God put this song on my heart. "Today is the day," by Lincoln Brewster! It's an upbeat song of praise.

Really?? Today is the day?

So I opened up youtube and pulled up the song and let it play.

*Today is the day, you have made, I will rejoice and be glad in it...*I didn't sing with it; not at first. I didn't agree with it. But something comforted and changed my heart towards the end of the song; I choked out the lyrics, "I won't worry about tomorrow; I'm giving you my fears and sorrows; where you lead me I will follow, trusting in what you say, Today is the Day."

We made the forty-minute drive to the hospital in Vancouver, WA. There were several friends and family around me. I wore my Cobras jersey to represent the "54club." I remember being taken to preop, wearing that drafty gown. There was peace in my heart and an acceptance of my fate. God certainly answered my prayers. It's hard to describe how it felt, but it reminded me of football. After you practice and do your film study you feel prepared; you feel ready to take the field. That's how I felt going into surgery.

The next thing I remember is waking up and seeing Leslie walk into my recovery room. I scratched my nose with my right hand and said, "Hey babe." The relieved look on her face was so comforting that I promptly went back to sleep.

After surgery we had to wait for pathology to find out what we were dealing with. We learned that my tumor was a malignant, grade 4, glioblastoma multiforme. This is an incurable cancer with just a 5-10% survival rate after 5 years of diagnosis. The goal of treatment is "to preserve as much of you for as long as possible." This was devastating news.

There are long term survivors with my kind of cancer. They are called "outliers." Fortunately, I had some things going for me that gave me a "great head start" (to quote my neurosurgeon); first, my tumor was encapsulated and he was able to remove 95-96% of it; it had a mutation that made it more susceptible to radiation; I'm young and had the energy to fight; and my health and fitness were good. My oncologist told me that I was "the fittest patient she'd had in 17 years of medical oncology!"

My team of doctors were amazing. I had arguably the best neurosurgeon in Northwest, and both my radiation and medical oncologists were Christians. God chose to use them to help bring about healing in my brain. The last meeting with my medical oncologist before our family moved, she said of my last scan, "It's either remission or cure, God only knows." At the time of this writing I have had 5 consecutive stable MRI scans. I believe and trust in the healing that Jesus brought about in my life.

I shared my story at Life Change Christian Fellowship on March 4th, 2018. After the service, my family was called to the front for prayer. The church gathered around me and began praying. In the middle of the prayer time I felt heat in my tumor site; it went from there down my neck all the way to my toes. I believe this is the moment that God fully healed me from cancer. My next scan was stable and there has been no trace of any lesions or enhancing tumors in my brain since then.

Throughout this entire ordeal, I've had God give me peace from Himself, or from people in His Church. My hope is that you can learn from my suffering how to get this peace. I have had to fully rely on God for deliverance. Maybe my struggles and lessons can help you in your life.

The fact that the idea for this book came after my surgery gives me hope that God's not done with me. It will give you a look into my life's darkest and most hopeless circumstance; it touches on parenting, trusting in God, and is a defense for my faith in Jesus Christ. It is my story.

Before we dive into my story, I must preface it with credit where credit is due. I want to share with you the true story that changed my life when I was 21 years old. It became the story of my life and the foundation of my marriage. This was the story that gave me the strength and courage possible to face down my incurable cancer. The main man in this story brought about a miraculous healing in my life. This is the story that saved my life. And as with every good story, there's a catchy beginning.

In the beginning God created the heavens and the earth. It was a perfect world. God created a beautiful garden with immortality in mind. In this garden He provided food and two amazing trees. One was called the Tree of Life, and the other was the Tree of the Knowledge of Good and Evil. God warned the first man and woman not to eat the fruit of the latter tree, 'for the day you eat of it you will surely die.'

We were created by God to live with Him forever, in the beginning. There was perfect peace, unity, and love. But the one threat to the perfect world was free will. Forcing your will on someone is not an act of love, but of aggression. God is love. So, He created humanity with the ability to choose. We have in ourselves the will to accept or reject anyone, including God. God set one condition for relationship with Him in the beginning, and He gave humans the choice to trust Him or not.

The devil came to the garden that God had made and tempted the woman to eat the forbidden fruit. He deceived her, saying she would become like God. Then she ate the fruit, then gave some to her husband. And he was with her the whole time; passive, and not protecting his bride.

This is called, The Fall.

Sin entered the world on account of the first humans on the planet. And they did eventually physically die. What was immediate after the first sin was a spiritual death that separated them from God. They were no longer innocent. As a young toddler is innocent and doesn't feel the shame of being naked, so the first humans used to be. But they were ashamed of their nakedness. And in the second generation of humanity, the first murder was committed on this new Creation.

God, however, was not defeated by the devil. The evil one could not foresee the plan of God because he himself is a created being. God, in His wisdom, had a game plan He set in motion at the fall, by killing an animal and providing clothes for the first human couple. This was the beginning of a system of sacrifices that would atone or cover the sins of people.

Eventually God appeared to a man named Abram. It is through the promise that God gave to Abram, later called Abraham, that the nation of Israel was born. And to this nation, God gave His law. Have no other gods beside Him. Don't covet your neighbors' possessions or spouse; theft, murder, adultery, sexual immorality, hatred, greed, and lying. God identified—labeled—sin.

In addition to labeling sin, He foreshadowed the plan He made in the beginning, that there would be a final sacrifice to atone for, to cover, sin. There was a national, annual event where the sins of the people could be forgiven in the nation of Israel. It took place on one day.

But it was an imperfect and incomplete forgiveness, because, what happens if you sin the following day? You had to wait an entire year to be atoned for! The descendants of Abraham had to go annually to make the same sacrifices, which couldn't fully remove or cover the sins of the people.

God, for His part, had to show that humanity *had* to turn to Him. If He didn't reveal His law to humanity, then the charge could be made that people didn't know any better, so how could they be at fault? And as we humans often do, we continue to struggle with sin.

When Jesus arrived on the scene some two thousand years ago, God made the big reveal of His plan. Check out Josh.org to see how utterly improbable and impossible it was for Jesus to fulfill all Old Testament Messianic Prophesies.

To quote Josh McDowell's website, "Peter Stoner, in his classic book Science Speaks, calculated the chance of any man fulfilling these prophesies, even down to the present time, to be 1 in 100,000,000,000,000,000 (10 to the 17th power)." (Sheri Bell, "Did Jesus Fulfill Old Testament Prophecy?", Josh McDowell Ministry; blog, posted March 28, 2018; https://www.josh.org/jesus-fulfill-prophesy/; accessed 12/10/2018).

In other words, it wasn't a coincidence. It wasn't by chance.

I challenge you to investigate the claims of the Bible. Be noble and honest with yourself. Is it a coincidence? Is life just an accident? If the Big Bang is the truth, how do you reconcile that with your personal life experience with explosions? When have you ever seen an explosion produce order or perfectly balanced structures? If molecules to man evolution is true, then how do you reconcile that with your personal life experience with information? When have you ever seen random selection produce anything resembling information, even simple information, let alone DNA?

Creation is proclaiming all around us that there is a Creator. We can see the vastness of space and the organization of tiny cells. It speaks to wisdom, creativity and order. This is called "general revelation."

Jesus Christ proclaimed Himself the Creator. He claimed to be one with God. His teachings are recorded in the New Testament of the Bible. He claimed to be God in the flesh and proved this by rising from the grave. This is called "special revelation."

"For I delivered to you as of first importance what I also received: that Christ died for our sins in accordance with the Scriptures, that he was buried, that he was raised on the third day in accordance with the Scriptures, and that he appeared to Cephas, then to the twelve. Then he appeared to more than five hundred brothers at one time, most of whom are still alive, though some have fallen asleep." (1 Corinthians 15:3-6 ESV)

I'm trusting in Christ, not only for healing today, but for resurrection from the dead tomorrow. Here's the bottom line: *"if there is no resurrection of the dead, then not even Christ has been raised."* (1 Corinthians 15:13)

I cannot deny the peace during my treatment. I can't deny the healing in my body and the strengthening to go back to work throughout my cancer treatments. There is no denying the body of work and the consistency of answered prayers in my life. And it all comes down to the resurrection of

Jesus: is it true or not? My life demonstrates it to be true!

Do you believe this? Do you believe that if you confess with your mouth that Jesus is Lord and believe in your heart that God raised Jesus from the dead that you'll be saved from death? Forgiven of your sin? Promised resurrection?

Lord Jesus, I confess I have sinned. I repent—turn away—from the evil way I lived before. I believe that you were raised from the dead. Now I call on you to be my Lord and Savior! Amen

People who die every day die easily.

In other words, coming to the end of life, those people are not scared, filled with sorrow and sadness.

Rather, they look to forward to Heaven with hope. This means I must live with death in mind.

To be absent from the body is to be present with the Lord.

BEFORE WE TAKE THE FIELD...

Living with Courage

"Precious in the sight of the LORD is the death of his saints." (Psalm 116:15 ESV)

As a believer in Jesus Christ, I have real hope. And I no longer fear death.

Not too long ago I was challenged to die daily through a devotion written by C. H. Spurgeon called "Dying Daily."[1]

---

[1] Charles Haddon Spurgeon, "Dying Daily," sermon, August 30, 1868, Metropolitan Tabernacle, Newington, UK; http://www.spurgeongems.org/vols13-15/chs828.pdf, accessed

He said that people who die every day die easily. In other words, coming to the end of life, those people are not scared, filled with sorrow and sadness. Rather, they look to forward to Heaven with hope.

This means I must live with death in mind.

It needs to be something that is a regular and natural part of conversation with others, particularly those in the faith. When we cross over through the Iron Gate of Death, as Spurgeon called it, we are not alone. To live is Christ; to die is gain. To be absent from the body is to be present with the Lord.

Father, give me courage to face death with my eternal life in mind.

Thank you for sending your Son, the Good Shepherd.

He will Shepherd me through life, through death, and through resurrection.

Amen.

12/10/2018.

CHAPTER 1 - FIRST QUARTER

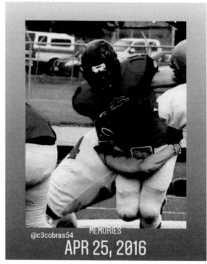

MEMORIES
@c3cobras54
APR 25, 2016

"Tackle for a Loss"
photo credit Brian Drake

Get in the Huddle
February 24, 2017
Listen to Advice
Proverbs 19:20-21 Listen to advice and accept
instruction, that you may gain wisdom in the future.
21 Many are the plans in the mind of a man, but it is
the purpose of the LORD that will stand.

One thing that having a brain tumor has
shown me is that, truly, I make a lot of plans. Tons of
them. I have plans for the church, for the football
team, for the family, for the marriage, and on and on.

But, the purpose of the Lord stands. Really, the truth is, all these plans are subject to God's will. God's purpose is to create in me a clean heart; it's to produce righteousness in my life. This means that my plans may not be the things carried out.

But, I know that God's purpose will stand! No matter the tumor, no matter the planning actions. He will finish His work in and thru my life.

This ties to the first part of this Proverb. Listening to advice and accepting instruction is like making long term banking deposits that pay you back later. For example, I've been planning some ministry work for several months; I've sought counsel, instruction, and prepared as best I could for it. The wisdom I gained laid the groundwork that built a bridge for people to be involved in the ministry I planned. I'm not able to do the plans I made. But the plans are being carried out, because at the end of the day it was God's purpose for that ministry to go on. His purpose will stand!

Lord, help me to listen to advice and accept instruction from others, especially those who are much wiser than me. I have so many plans, but I surrender them all to Your will and I want forever in my life, Your purpose to stand. Amen.

Reflections and personal notes:_____

_____
_____
_____
_____

Get in the Huddle
February 25, 2017
Forget Happiness?
Lamentations 3:21 But this I call to mind, and
therefore I have hope.

In Lamentations 3, the writer laid out his
complaint before God. He felt trapped, robbed, and
treated unjustly. God, you took my strength. You
took my security! I have no endurance for this work;
my hope is gone; I forgot how to be happy.

Can you imagine what it feels like to come to
a place, "I have forgotten what happiness is?"

The first 20 verses bear out this incredible
suffering. Maybe you're there. Maybe you're facing
a trial that you just can see past.

Well, the play-call here is simple—something
to call to mind. The writer did this and then his entire
perspective changed.

The first thought to change his despair was:
"The steadfast love of the LORD never ceases; his
mercies never come to an end; they are new every
morning; great is your faithfulness."

He goes on about God's goodness, His track
record with his people. Check out the rest of the
verses:

"It is good that one should wait quietly for
the salvation of the LORD. It is good for a man that
he bear the yoke in his youth. Let him sit alone in
silence when it is laid on him; let him put his mouth
in the dust—there may yet be hope; let him give his
cheek to the one who strikes and let him be filled

with insults. For the LORD will not cast off forever, but, though he cause grief, he will have compassion according to the abundance of his steadfast love; for he does not afflict from his heart or grieve the children of men."

He continues on in this reciting of God's justice, His creative power and summarizes it this way: "Why should a living man complain, a man, about the punishment of his sins?"

God, let us test and examine our ways, and return to the LORD! Let us lift up our hearts and hands to God in heaven. Hear our cry for help; come near when we call; forgive us our sins, O God! You've seen our plight and have mercy. Amen.

Reflections and personal notes:_____

_____

_____

_____

_____

_____

_____

_____

_____

_____

Get in the Huddle
February 26, 2017
Don't be Afraid to Ask
Proverbs 19:20 Listen to advice and accept
instruction, that you may gain wisdom in the future.

Don't be afraid to ask someone in your life,
"what do you think about this with me?" One thing
that I struggle with is saying 'No' to things. I love to
help others, to serve and to make a difference. There
is an older man I have recently met and I could tell
that he has had some things he wanted to tell me, but
is just respectful and kind enough that he wouldn't
offer it to me unsolicited.

This past year or so before I found out about
my tumor, my life schedule has been a hectic wreck.
Two jobs, a nonprofit organization, and so on. Plus, a
marriage, seven kids, and a workout schedule at 5a,
or workouts don't happen.

I could see what was happening to me, but I
needed someone to tell me straight. Someone willing
to take a risk.

First thing: inventory your relationships—are
there older men or women in your life that you look
up to for their service to God and success in family?
Second thing: would it be the end of the world if you
approached them and just said, "Could I get some
advice?" That in no way dishonors God. It's not
weakness. A man who thinks he has it figured out is
a fool. No one was made to face life alone, despite
our fanatical romanticism in the USA with the

Superman hero-type (ya, we got support staff, but in the end, we got this).

I got my advice and it was hard to hear; but I have put the advice into practice. I've stepped down from a couple areas of my life that were good things, and have decided not to pursue them. God has a better purpose for me than always being tired and in need of rest. So, I'll trust Him, even if the money is tighter and even if it means I have to listen to somebody's advice.

God, help me to listen and accept advice. I want to have wisdom in the future and just experience the fruit of wisdom from the rich life experience you have graciously given to others. Amen.

Reflections and personal notes:_____

_____

_____

_____

_____

_____

_____

_____

_____

_____

Get in the Huddle
March 06, 2017
Head on a Swivel!
Galatians 6:1 Brothers, if anyone is caught in any transgression, you who are spiritual should restore him in a spirit of gentleness. Keep watch on yourself, lest you too be tempted.

One thing you learn quickly on the football field is to keep your head on a swivel. If you don't know what that means, well, maybe you're not ready for contact! I've been on the receiving end of one or two monster hits in my football career just because I wasn't watching like I should have been. One play stands out in particular the 2016 season. We were playing the Renegades in southern Oregon. We had the offense pinned back to the goal, and it was an obvious run situation.

The snap, the read, the reaction. It was a toss left with a full back lead blocker; the line blocked down. I started scraping to my left, looking for open doors to shut. I spotted the lead fullback, Alvin Thornton, and he looked like he was going to keep pressing left for the edge. Our pursuit and angles were good and the running back was getting corralled. I glanced back inside and made a move thru an open door to assist with the tackle. Instead, I got smashed by that full back who I thought was heading farther out. He knew the play was beat, but still wheeled back and dipped into me. It was the hardest shoulder block I've ever felt. The hit didn't take me down, but it took me by complete surprise!

Believe me, that the next play I was looking for him a head up collision; if I didn't know any better, he didn't want a head up collision! "The tape evidence don't lie!" In all seriousness, he got me pretty good the previous play because I didn't have my head on a swivel.

Alvin Thornton's big hit - photo credit Brian Drake

God, help me to keep my head on a swivel in life. Help me not to be caught off guard by sin and to be ready at all times to face temptations. Amen.

Reflections and personal notes:_____

_____

_____

_____

_____

TIMEOUT – The Cowlitz Cobras

Photo credit Brian Drake

A few years ago, a minor league football team popped up in Longview, WA. It was called the Cowlitz County Blackhawks. I heard they were having a tryout and were looking for players. This happened not long after I brought Fathers in the Field to Castle Rock (there is a timeout entry in the 4th quarter about this). When I considered going out for the team, my first thought was, "Yes! I love football; lets' go!" Football is a reflection of life and the lessons that can be learned from it. But, over the years I've learned to slow down the decision-making process.

The truth was, I couldn't justify going to play football without having a compelling "why." I thought of fatherless boys that were being left to become men without a mentor or a role model. Many of these men were now having sons of their own, but were struggling to figure out this manhood and fatherhood thing. Most of the players didn't have dads. So, I had my "why." I figured I could mentor younger guys and have a blast playing the game I love. I decided to check it out. It became a six-month ordeal that saw me break a finger, establish some mentoring relationships, and be the heart and soul of the defense.

The next year I started a 501 (c)3 non-profit organization called the Cowlitz (County) Cobras. I developed a mission and vision statement that guided the organization side of the team. My vision was building community champions. The mission was to "advance the participation of organized football beyond the secondary and post-secondary school levels and to pursue excellence on and off the field."

We built community champions by giving players a chance to compete for scholarships, by developing football skills and providing film, tryouts for nearby arena and professional teams throughout the United States. The players, coaches and staff of the Cobras were expected to take a role in serving and blessing the community. Community champions protected neighborhoods, helped others, and built healthy communities thru volunteer service. We worked to hold each other accountable and tried to take responsibility for our actions.

Community champions used football as a point of contact for mentoring and encouragement of boys and men of all ages, including the growing fatherless population. Players, staff, and coaches were required to adhere to my zero-tolerance alcohol and other drug policy while publicly representing the organization. I envisioned a team of players that would be invested in their communities and would be change partners, or agents, in their spheres of influence.

The Cowlitz Cobras always accomplished the vision of building and being community champions. From working with Habitat for Humanity and serving at the Community House Homeless Shelter, to being guest speakers at the local Cub Scouts and Goodwill's At Risk Youth program, and practicing at a local park in our community, we carried out the vision.

In 2016 we partnered with Cowlitz County Veterans Services, raising $200 for them during Military Appreciation Night home game; at half-time we honored those who served in the military on our team, and acknowledged those who served our country in the stands.

Several players on my team gave back to the community by coaching youth football, from Pop Warner to High School (K-12). For 3 years running the Cowlitz Cobras conducted a heads-up tackling clinic/demonstration for Lower Columbia Youth Football Association at Mt. Solo Middle School. This league would later include our Little Cobras football team. We also sponsored, and I coached, a Little Cobras youth soccer team.

At our home finale in 2016 we hosted our 2nd Annual Fight Like A Girl "Pink Out: Team Claudia" where we raised just over $700 for Claudia and her family (she was battling breast cancer). We feel blessed and fortunate to have had the opportunity to be a part of helping send Claudia and her family on a dream vacation. Claudia lost her fight not long after the trip, and the annual fundraiser became a memorial game and we still encouraged every player, from both teams, to participate in the "pink-out" part of the game.

Also, in 2016, the Cowlitz Cobras hosted the I Topped The Rock 5k race in Castle Rock, getting 56 participants. We raised for Cowlitz County Veterans Services an additional $105 at this event.

I wanted to show our community that we were all in with the vision and mission. As I mentioned, I moved our practices to an abandoned city park called Archie Anderson Park, where we hoped to one day build a home stadium for the Cowlitz Cobras.

The city council was in favor of it. I was in initial planning meetings for a new site plan for the park that included a football field and training facility for the Cobras; I secured a matching grant for goalposts and a scoreboard to start the process. I even had a local architect donate time to draw up a rough site plan for the field (complete with the Cobras logo on the 50!)

Unfortunately, my passion and vision weren't fulfilled, as I couldn't raise the funds while going through chemo treatments. God clearly closed the door on my dream to build a stadium in Longview.

Still, the Cobras accomplished the vision of building community champions in our community. We worked with habitat for humanity, were members of the chamber of commerce in two cities, served at the homeless shelter (Community House on Broadway), participated annually in the National Night Out, supported and mentored the local cub scout pack in the Highlands neighborhood (including letting them do concessions at the home games to raise money for camp), and had many, many local sponsors.

This doesn't count the personal sacrifice of time, talent and treasure it took to run the team. It cost thousands of dollars. Hundreds of hours. Gallons of blood, sweat, and tears. OK; OK; it was mostly sweat, some tears, and a little bit of blood.

After I got sick with cancer, I couldn't keep up with the fundraising or leading the organization. It was a struggle to keep up with the demands of the team while I trudged through recovery from surgery, radiation, and chemotherapy. I needed to pass on the torch and walk away.

I am proud and happy to report that the Cobras finished a fourth season. They continued to build community champions. Unfortunately, the league they were a member of folded. The Cobras have been shelved for the foreseeable future.

This experience showed me that God gives you the desires of your heart when you seek His kingdom first. And I learned that you may have the right vision, but not the right timing. You can have the right timing, but not be the one to carry out the vision.

I long desired to play tackle football; I have compassion for fatherless boys and young men; I want to make and see a positive difference in my community. God used me. I'm so grateful to have been able to serve God through football. If I can do it, surely you can do something to make a change in your community.

My prayer is that you are finding this book to be encouraging. I want God to use it to strengthen you in your walk with Christ.

I want you to find hope and rest in the fact that God is good. Even when you get rocked with a blindside block with news like, "You've got a brain tumor." Let my story remind you that God is there and is not silent.

This has forced me to wrestle with suffering and affliction that happens to God's people. I've had to learn how to have joy through sorrow & pain. Jesus has proven Himself strong in my life, through provision, peace, & healing.

What's at stake for me is, can God be trusted? Does He tell people the truth, even today? Does He still speak through prophets today? Does He still heal today? Does He assure and reassure me only to pull the rug out from me later?

I'm glad you are reading this with me. Keep going; get back in the huddle.

Get in the Huddle
March 08, 2017
Painted Rocks
Isaiah 26:4 Trust in the LORD forever, for the
LORD GOD is an everlasting rock.

There is a new group popped up in Cowlitz
County a few months ago. If I'm not mistaken, it is
completely started and communicated about thru the
social media giant Facebook. They are rock painters;
here they are called, "Cowlitz County Rocks!"

People gather rocks, paint them, mark them
on the back "Cowlitz County Rocks," put a little "f"
for Facebook on it, then go hide them throughout the
county. You're supposed to take pics of the rocks
when you hide and find them, then share on the
group page, or on your page. It's a pretty fun craft
and I think open-source, starfish type organizations
like this are pretty awesome like that.

One of my students made one for me after she
heard about my brain tumor and she gave it to me. It
says, "Mr. Royce Rocks!" So I went and hid it
yesterday. I've been able to share my story with
more people because my little friend painted a rock
for me!

God is an everlasting rock. His message for
you is painted in the blood of His Son, Jesus Christ.
While my rock is temporary, eventually the paint will
wear off, not so with the blood of Christ; it etches
our rock of salvation forever. It is permanent. You
are permanently covered by the blood of Jesus
Christ; trust in Him.

27

Father, thank you for being an everlasting rock of salvation. Help me to trust in you forever, amen.

Reflections and personal notes:_____
_____
_____
_____
_____
_____
_____
_____
_____
_____

Get in the Huddle
March 11, 2017
Words of Life!
Ezekiel 37:4 Then he said to me, "Prophesy over these bones, and say to them, O dry bones, hear the word of the LORD."

Even death listens to the Word of the Lord. Nothing can stand against the Word of the Lord. In the beginning was the Word! In the beginning, God said, let there be light. Nothing that comes out of God's mouth can be overturned, overruled, overpowered or changed.

If God speaks vision, peace and direction to your heart, it is yours! He says, come to me, all who are weary and heavy laden, and I will give you rest. So, if you are weary and heavy laden, Christian, why don't you do what his Word tells you? Get with Him! For me, it's called "Knee time! Because there I find less of me time."

Father, help me to listen to and trust in Your Word! You are speaking to death words of life! Let my dry bones hear Your word today, in Jesus' name, amen.

Reflections and personal notes:_____

_____
_____
_____
_____
_____

PENALTY FLAG – SIN

stock photo

You've shed your blocker, dipped the shoulder, and ripped under the outside of the right tackle. You have a straight shot at the quarterback who is looking to the left, head turned away from you. Finally, you have a shot at a game-changing play. In a moment you're launched into the air and you hit the quarterback so hard, the ball is knocked loose; with under 2 minutes to go in the game, defending the goal, just 24 yards to the endzone, your team recovers the game sealing fumble and you begin to celebrate the close but inevitable victory. The offense begins to run onto the field for the victory formation. The shout is caught in your throat as you look and see a yellow flag in the area of the quarterback, who is slowly rising to his feet, pumping his fist.

"Personal foul, roughing the passer—helmet to helmet, number 93, 15 yard penalty, automatic first down."

Sometimes, penalties completely change the outcome of the football game. This was a familiar, albeit hypothetical, narrative for many a player and fan. The opposing team capitalizes on the mistake and goes on to win the game.

I compare penalties to sins in our lives. Sometimes they are not intended; they are mistakes; lapses in judgment or focus, the 5 yard penalty variety. Other times, penalties are for unsportsmanlike conduct or fighting. This, to me, is a good parallel to the sin in our lives.

If you have sinned against your neighbor, be it your actual neighbor, your spouse, your kid(s), your family, your boss, etc, then you have committed a penalty. Every penalty carries a cost, and sometimes this cost can dramatically alter the game; even lose you the game.

Seeking forgiveness
Relationship penalties can be minor or egregious. Either way, here are some steps to seek forgiveness:
1. Pray, asking God to humble your heart.
2. Confess your sin to God; seek forgiveness from Him. Repent—turn away from your sin.
3. Confess your sin to the person in question; seek forgiveness from them. Repent—turn away from that sin; pay restitution if necessary.

Offering forgiveness
The person on the receiving end of this also has some steps to grant forgiveness:

1.	Realize that no sin committed against you compares to the evil laid on Jesus (the sin of the entire world; every.single.sin on the cross.); He <u>DOES</u> understand how you feel.
2.	Forgive the person who sinned against you* before they seek it; develop compassion for that person.
3.	Accept the apology and forgive.

*Keeping the peace**
If the reconciliation is legitimate, then there are ground rules, or promises, that are to be kept.
I promise:
1.	Not to dwell on the incident(s).
2.	Not to use the incident(s) against them.
3.	When I remember their sin against me, I will offer forgiveness again, following the example of Jesus Christ.

*if you are experiencing domestic violence contact the local authorities and report it. Remove yourself from the dangerous situation. Use wisdom, and get professional help. Irrespective of the situation, you must forgive, even if you've been abused; God will forgive us as we have forgiven others. Offering forgiveness is not the same as rebuilding trust or creating boundaries for safety. Forgiveness will bring about freedom in your heart.

Get in the Huddle
March 13, 2017
Finding Strength
Ephesians 6:10 Finally, be strong in the Lord and in the strength of his might.

The real deal is hard to find. Have you noticed that true friends are in short supply? Why are they hard to find? I think this is because there is only 1 person who will always be there. Be strong in the Lord and in his mighty power. Not your best friend. Not your wife. Not your kid. Not yourself. Not your drug. Not your pre-workout. Not your plan.
Jesus.
You get strong in Jesus.
You stay strong in His mighty power.
What power?
Strength for today and hope for tomorrow.
Period.
God, I will be strong in You. Bring victory and power to bear in my life so that I can be strong, and not for strength sake, but for you. To be strong in You. Amen.

Reflections and personal notes:_____
_____
_____
_____
_____
_____

Get in the Huddle
March 14, 2017
Faith Shield
Ephesians 6:16 In all circumstances take up the shield of faith, with which you can extinguish all the flaming darts of the evil one.

Have you ever met someone who ignored problems? Or swept them under the rug? This is a very dangerous proposition in your spiritual life. You have a blind spot, but you know about it (you know, the swimsuit issue isn't porn, chill!). You have doubts that you are forgiven and have fear that God is just looking for an opportunity to nail you about it.

Flaming arrows of the evil one destroy people. They burn up peace and comfort. They consume joy.

You must not ignore them! Other flaming arrows, like, you'll never change; you'll never be good enough; you'll never make it; you screwed up for the last time; these can't be ignored. They must be extinguished! Not by ignoring them in the air. Not by running away from them either!

No, man of God; STAND your ground; face those flaming arrows, and extinguish them with the shield of faith!

How this works is you see them, you acknowledge them, then you raise your faith.

I believe that God's word is true, therefore I will turn my eyes from worthless things; I admit lust is lust and confess it as sin. God demonstrated his own love for me in that while I was still a sinner,

Christ died for me. My eternal life, my inheritance, is totally sealed and guaranteed by the Holy Spirit who was given to me after I placed my faith in Jesus Christ for salvation. I have been forgiven. God is a good father and His plans for me are for my good. Jesus keeps His promise, and will therefore continue changing and refining me for His good works, for the praise of His glory.

God, help me to face the danger to my soul today. Give me courage, first to stand my ground, and second, give me strength to raise my shield of faith. Thank you, amen.

Reflections and personal notes:_____

_____

_____

_____

_____

_____

_____

_____

_____

_____

CHALLENGE FLAG! – CREATION vs.
"The universe is billions of years old."

stock photo

Our culture accepts that the universe is billions of years old; it's a culture axiom that dinosaurs lived millions of years ago. We use the term dinosaur to emphatically refer to older things.

This challenge flag is an apologetic for the age of the earth.

The main question I have about long ages is, how could anyone possibly know that? People who hold this view rely on HUGE assumptions to come to their position. We can't observe scientifically anything in the distant past.

Dating methods rely on the assumption that decay rates are constant, unchanging, into the distant past; as far as how old things are, how much of the matter/material/elements in rocks were there to begin with? Maybe ask the question, what effect does lava's heat have on the decay rates within rocks, especially hardening as they cool? Why can't current dating methods arrive at an accurate date for the rock formation caused by Mt St Helens in Washington state? How is there still helium in diamonds?

Speaking of Mt St Helens in Washington state, Castle Rock is the gateway to the volcano. Did you know there is a creation museum/center in the city of Castle Rock? The director is Paul Taylor, and he leads excursions exploring the mountain. The center provides extremely compelling evidence related to Creationism. There are many free resources; Paul Taylor is an internationally respected speaker on Creation and he would love to see you! Tell him I sent you.

The earth's crust has been shaped violently in the past; the worldwide evidence suggests major volcanic activity. Did you know that the flood of Noah can account for the world we see today? Reminds me of a kid song: *if there ever was a world-wide flood, what would the evidence be? Billions of dead things, buried in rock layers, laid down by water, all over the earth!* What do we see today?

There are more than 200 flood myths and legends all around the world! So, cultures all around the world, that never knew each other, somehow all had this ancient myth and legend in common.

Regarding the big bang theory, I cannot accept that an explosion created the perfectly balanced and ordered universe we can observe today. Again, is there a single example of an explosion creating order or creating something? Didn't the myth busters take on the exploding paint myth that was all about the walls getting painted? Maybe explosion to carve granite, like say in South Dakota with Mount Rushmore or Crazyhorse can create order! Totally carved by explosions. Ah; no; never mind; these are carefully planned, designed, controlled and coordinated explosions. Not by chance. Not by accident.

Do you personally ever see randomness produce information? Could you randomly write Get in the Huddle for me? Could you write a short, coherent essay by randomly grabbing scrabble tiles out of a bag?

Obviously, you can't. But, if I wanted to convince you that randomness could produce my story, I would feed you a line about how long it takes to be written on its' own, by chance. And then I would silence my editor and family to make sure they can't tell you that I wrote it.

As impossible as that all sounds, people still try to feed the public that an explosion created the universe. The equation for the big bang theory is: Nothing + Nothing + Time (lots of time) x explosion = balanced and ordered universe! And how do we know?

One of the major assumptions about the big bang theory is that the universe has no center, or edge. How could we possibly know that to be true? Did you know that the Earth's location in the milky way galaxy makes observing the known universe possible? Coincidence? Or does Creation proclaim the glory of God, as His Word says?

Honest question to you: have you ever considered the claims of creation science? I would challenge you to do so and commend to you a few websites for further study and research:

- creation.com
- answersingensis.org
- mshcreationcenter.org
- icr.org
- arkencounter.com
- creationminute.com
- isgenesishistory.com

Get in the Huddle
March 18, 2017
God Meets Needs
Philippians 4:19 And my God will supply every need of yours according to his riches in glory in Christ Jesus.

This last Wednesday, I got a concerned call from my teenage son. He called on his older sister's behalf. They were having some significant car trouble. My wife and I were heading back from Vancouver, where we just finished our errands after my radiation treatment.

The crazy thing is, not 2 weeks ago, we had the car tuned up and checked out at the local shop. It had a clean bill of health. So, when he said that Nicki is flooring it but the RPMs won't go above 3,000 rpms, I told them to find a safe place to park it so it could be towed.

We were still 10 minutes from home.

I called AAA, found out that we had to add my daughter to be towed. After a tense few minutes of getting a tow truck arranged, we had the car taken back to the local shop. We prayed.

Then the call came in. It has a completely blocked catalytic converter, and because it is part of a single unit, it requires a total exhaust replacement. $810 and some change. We prayed.

Yesterday (Friday), I went to the school where I used to be a teacher (Three Rivers Christian School) to visit the 1st grade class (I was the K-7 PE and 6th Grade Bible Teacher), because their teacher said they raised some money for me and wanted to show me the big math problem they learned to count all the change.

So, I headed to the school; as I was walking out of the office with the 1st grade teacher, one of the HS teachers handed me an envelope with my name on it. I said thank you, then folded it up, following Ms. Woodman out the door to the classroom. I got to share a little bit about my treatment with the kids, then showed them my huge scar, and a couple pictures of my radiation setup. After that, we prayed together, and they blessed my heart so much; their prayers made me cry (but not much, because I'm tough). And they raised $16.35 for me!

Later, I opened the envelope. It was a love offering for $800.

God, thank you that you meet all our needs according to the riches of your glory in Christ Jesus. Amen.

Reflections and personal notes:_____

_____
_____
_____
_____
_____
_____
_____
_____
_____

Get in the Huddle
March 20, 2017
God's Ways
Micah 4:2   And many nations shall come, and say: "Come, let us go up to the mountain of the LORD, to the house of the God of Jacob, that he may teach us his ways and that we may walk in his paths." For out of Zion shall go forth the law, and the word of the LORD from Jerusalem.

How many people do you know that want to know God's plan for their life? Do you?

It never ceases to amaze me how people want the blessings of walking with God, but they don't accept that it's not all about that blessing. God has determined ways and paths for us to walk on. These may or may not include the rich blessings of God material favor.

There's a song by The Akins called "What if God says no?"

"What if God says no; it don't mean He loves you less; it just means He knows what's best, ooh; what if God says no, it's enough we have His grace, so don't let go of your faith, what if God says no."

My favorite part of the song is when it points out that God the Father said no to His Son in the Garden of Gethsemane.

Trials and challenges are coming; attacks from enemies, hatred from the world, destruction from Satan; all this is a part of life. Don't pretend that because you know God that He is going to just make everything trial free! His path is narrow, and level. You can walk on it. The amazing thing about all the ugly things that happen in life is that while walking with God, He makes everything beautiful. Even if He answers your prayers with a no, He is still working everything together for your good.

The text today has a very practical application for how you find God's ways and path—go up to the mountain; this means His presence. Get with other Christians and pray. Read the word of God because from Him flows His word; His truth. That's what you need; not the material blessings! And finally, realize that God's answers to your prayers are always yes, no or not yet! Be ok with His ways, paths, and answers.

Heavenly Father, I seek you on your mountain today; teach me your ways and paths so that I can have peace with the direction of my life. Amen.

Reflections and personal notes:_____
_____
_____
_____
_____
_____
_____
_____
_____
_____

Get in the Huddle
March 22, 2017
Joy and Peace
Psalm 30:5   For his anger is but for a moment, and his favor is for a lifetime. Weeping may tarry for the night, but joy comes with the morning.

My daughter Grace is the youngest of 7 children. She has had to learn to ask boldly and speak up to be heard around the house. She is very outgoing and extroverted. So, you can imagine, she is the one who asks the awkward questions and points out things to strangers that probably should be kept to herself. But hey, who can get mad at such a cute delivery from a 5 year old?

Last night she essentially demanded my time. And that is fine; it has been busy with appointments and people coming and going to my house. At the time of this writing it's just 37 days since my brain resection. She wanted to play barbies. So, we played barbies. I was shirtless batman, because apparently he needs to do his laundry! And batgirl is his wife; so we played practicing fighting the crimes of Dirty House and Not Working Out.

Then out of left field she asked me, "if after you go to see Jesus will you come back and be my daddy again?"

It hit me pretty hard; yesterday afternoon we got the news that my brain tumor is not receptive to the chemo options available to me. That is, over time it develops resistance to the chemo. Unless God heals me miraculously, it's a matter of time before this tumor kills me.

I snuggled up with Grace and told her that I would be here as long as I could be and I would always love her, no matter what. So we played more barbies, and then went to snuggle on the couch before she went to bed.

This morning I wept my eyes out in sorrow; then Jesus met me and comforted me! He comes to my rescue! I may be fighting for my life, but He is everything that is beautiful! A friend messaged me on Facebook this morning with a word of encouragement as I was praying on my knees; "stand tall today, brother." How did Curtis know I needed to hear that?

So that's what I'm doing! And "Manifesto" is blasting in my headphones as I write this. Amen! God set me free from sin and death. I see my path is to prepare Grace as much as I can to face life without me. Isn't that parenting anyway? Aren't all parents in the place of preparing their kids to live life without them? It just means that I may be 'sending her out' without me a little sooner than most. My joy comes from knowing that I have a chance today to prepare Grace for life, as well as my family! I have a purpose.

Father, thank you for comforting me. Thank you that your joy that DOES come in the morning. You give rest to the weary. I ask for your will to be done today in my life, amen.

Reflections and personal notes:_____

_____
_____
_____
_____
_____
_____
_____
_____
_____

Joel and Leslie, Tennessee, 2018

Get in the Huddle
March 23, 2017
Don't Isolate Yourself
Proverbs 18:1   Whoever isolates himself seeks his own desire; he breaks out against all sound judgment.

This verse is sometimes one of those that I have a hard time buying in dealing with conflict situations with my wife. We will be in an argument and I'll get frustrated and walk away angry, not wanting to keep talking. I want to get away from the tension and the stuff I don't want to deal with.

The truth is this shows a lack of control over my anger. It also reveals that I am not truly listening.

The sound judgment in a marital conflict is to seek to understand *rather* than be understood. If I truly understand where my wife is coming from then isolating my self is not something that happens. What happens to me when I really listen and understand her is that I'm able to see where she is coming from and I can work to find points of agreement. Compassion for her is something that definitely rises up when I really understand her.

It feels unnatural to press into a conflict and not isolate. There are lots of things people isolate themselves over, not just marital conflicts. Take this proverb by faith and don't isolate yourself. Reach out for help. Call someone and share what you're dealing with; go grab some coffee and share; if you isolate yourself you cut yourself off from advice, perspective, and help.

God, help me accept your word as truth; I will not isolate myself from your church or my bride; I will embrace sound judgment and not just seek my own desire! Amen.

Reflections and personal notes:_____

_____
_____
_____
_____
_____
_____
_____
_____
_____

CHAPTER 2- SECOND QUARTER

Joel on the far left

Get in the Huddle
March 26, 2017
Respect the Game
Matthew 24:12   And because lawlessness will be increased, the love of many will grow cold.

When you don't care about the rules, you don't care about others.

In football, it's easy to see which guys have respect for the game. They adhere to the rules; they are good sports. They don't make a big deal about themselves on the field. They listen to their coach.

Are they pushovers? Absolutely not! They stand their ground. Do they get penalties? Yes. Personal fouls? Perhaps occasionally.

A player that doesn't respect the game is also easy to spot. He'll take cheap shots. He'll mouth off at the refs, coaches, opponents and teammates. You can't tell a guy like this anything.

The deep respect I have for the game comes from a deep love for the game. The same is true for people. Respect for the rule of law is grounded in a love for your fellow man. Show me a rioter, and I'll show you someone who doesn't respect or love others.

God, don't let my love grow cold. Even if everyone around me should throw off all laws and rules, I will love You and I will love my neighbor. Amen.

Reflections and personal notes:_____

_____
_____
_____
_____
_____
_____
_____
_____
_____

Get in the Huddle
March 27, 2017
Heart
Psalm 86:11 Teach me your way, O LORD, that I may walk in your truth; unite my heart to fear your name.

A heart that is not united can be several things. Distracted. Broken. Vengeful. Hardened. Carried away. Ill-intentioned. Double-minded. Anxious.

A heart that is united is devoted. It's singularly focused on one thing.

This Psalm serves as a prayer in my life sometimes. I want to learn God's way for my life; His path; my next steps. Teach me the way to go, O God! Because when I learn your way, I can walk in Your truth. How can I walk in God's truth if He doesn't teach me His way?

This means that I must dedicate myself to reading the bible, first with a prayer of a student— teach me Your way, O Lord. God's ways are taught in the scriptures.

God, help me to be a student of Your Word; I will apply myself to learning Your way. I want to walk in Your truth every day, Father. Unite my heart from everything that distracts it from You. I give your name respect, honor and the glory it is due. Amen.

Reflections and personal notes:_____

_____

_____

_____

_____

_____

_____

_____

_____

_____

_____

Get in the Huddle
March 28, 2017
God of the Living Dead
Romans 14:8-9   For if we live, we live to the Lord,
and if we die, we die to the Lord. So then, whether
we live or whether we die, we are the Lord's. [9] For to
this end Christ died and lived again, that he might be
Lord both of the dead and of the living.

The fact that Jesus is Lord both of the dead
and the living brings me great comfort. Whatever
happens to me, I am His. If I die today, or if I die in
80 years, I am His. This is a peaceful place to be.
There is no hopeless wonder of what happens after
death for me.

There are some certain things in life. For
example, I am certain that I am married to Leslie;
I'm certain that I love her; I'm certain that she loves
me. I am certain that God exists and Jesus rose from
the dead. I'm certain that I love Him; I'm certain that
He loves me. It's no more arrogant to claim that I
know beyond a shadow of a doubt that God exists
and that Jesus rose from the dead than it is for me to
say that I know that Leslie is my bride and that we
live together. Jesus *answers* my prayers. He bears *my*
burdens of fear and doubt about my cancer.

I live to the Lord! As I seek Him and get
closer to Him I get strength; I get peace. He isn't just
there at the end of life to deal with the fact that "I'm
going up to the Spirit in the sky." He's also there
right now. He is Lord in my life right now; and like

any good leader, He checks in on His people; the people He leads are well cared for.

Jesus, thank you that you are Lord of the dead and of the living! You're not merely a comfort and leader for death; you are Lord and leader in life. I humble myself to your leading today, come what may. Amen.

Reflections and personal notes:_____

_____
_____
_____
_____
_____
_____
_____
_____
_____

Get in the Huddle
March 29, 2017
God of Hope
Romans 15:13   May the God of hope fill you with all joy and peace in believing, so that by the power of the Holy Spirit you may abound in hope.

A few days ago I went to make coffee in the kitchen. I put in the grounds, water, and hit 'brew.' Since I get up really early these days I have time to study the Word, pray, and write before I have to interact with anyone in the house (other than the occasional whiny pooch that needs to go outside!).

This particular morning I made a mistake in brewing my coffee. I neglected to empty the carafe, which was over half full from the previous pot of coffee that was brewed. Needless to say, the coffee overflowed! It made a huge mess on the counter and the floor.

This is kinda the idea in this passage I shared "so that by the power of the Holy Spirit you may abound in hope." Other translations capture the idea of 'overflowing.' This is the idea of abounding here in the text. It means, overflowing in hope—much like my carafe. Getting everywhere, not discriminating between paper that may be on the counter and glass pans that are water proof.

This passage is also a prayer from the apostle Paul to the church; we'd do well to pray this scripture over ourselves, families, friends, pastors, and so on.

God is a God of hope; and by the power of the Holy Spirit, we can overflow with hope. This hope comes from joy and peace. You can bet that this is what I have experienced so far in my cancer fight; I have joy and peace. Joy knowing that God is glorified in my story and that I am doing His will; peace in knowing that Christ is Lord of life and death; He's with me and gives me strength; He quiets my soul and comforts my sorrow. It's peace I can't explain. And the end result of it all is *hope*. My hope overflows! There are times I just share my story with people that didn't expect to hear it.

Let me warn you: if we should meet in person and you ask me the question, "How are you," be prepared for me to share a little more than the usual, "I'm doing good."

God, may you fill me and the reader with all joy and peace in believing, so that by the power of the Holy Spirit we may overflow in hope! Amen.

Reflections and personal notes:_____

_____
_____
_____
_____
_____
_____
_____
_____
_____

Get in the Huddle
March 30, 2017
Ripe on the Vine
Song of Solomon 2:13   The fig tree ripens its figs,
and the vines are in blossom; they give forth
fragrance. Arise, my love, my beautiful one, and
come away.

I love fruit. Ripe fruit is the best. Maybe it's
the sugar in it, but regardless, I have never met a ripe
fruit I didn't enjoy eating, even the sour ones! Going
to the store to grab fruits and veggies is actually
something I enjoy doing. When I go past the oranges
and they're ripe, I always take a deep breath to smell
that citrussy goodness.

One thing that bothers me about store bought
fruit is the knowledge that little or none of it was
ripened on the branch or vine. Bananas are solid
green when they are picked from the tree. While you
may be able to ripen physical fruit off the tree or the
vine, you can't do this with spiritual fruit.

Maybe it's because our culture has a 'fast-
food' mentality when it comes to what we need. I
ordered it, and now I shouldn't have to wait long
(next day shipping from anywhere, please!). Perhaps
the reason is we want the results and the glory for
making it happen. So, we ripen the fruit off the vine,
then we get glory for the good taste of it.

The problem is spiritual fruit will not ripen
off the vine. If you pluck it early, you don't have it.
The fruit of the Spirit is love, joy, peace, patience,
kindness, goodness, faithfulness, gentleness, and

self-control. These things can't be picked until they are ripe! In other words, you must pray until you have them. You must yield your heart to God until these fruits ripen on the vine. This means it may take you longer than 5 minutes of praying in the morning. Would you be willing to wait on the Lord for peace longer than that? How long would you wait on the Lord for the fruit of the Spirit?

Father, I commit today to not leave this posture of prayer until the fruit of the Spirit is ripe for me to pluck. I don't want the glory for trying to ripen these good fruits apart from you; to Your name be all the glory, in Jesus' name, amen.

Reflections and personal notes:_____
_____
_____
_____
_____
_____
_____
_____
_____
_____

Get in the Huddle
April 06, 2017
Run the Race
1 Corinthians 9:24   Do you not know that in a race all the runners run, but only one receives the prize? So run that you may obtain it.

I use to think this was a comparative passage. Other runners versus me. This led to some discouragement. How can I run the race like that guy?

This was immature thinking. Paul is making the point that the goal is the prize. The prize is our reward in heaven. You *can* be the winner of your race because you are the only one that can run *your* race.

You and I have a race that is marked out for us individually. No one can run our race like us. And we must win the race in our own lives.

Hebrews 12:1 (MPTV—My Personal Translation Version) says drop the junk you keep hauling around and turn away from the sin that keeps screwing things up so you can run your race!

Compete! Don't give up. Don't suffer loss in your own race.

God, help me to run in such a way as to win the prize in my race. Help me to realize that by laying down my burdens and turning from my sin that I am in first place—and help me maintain my position until I die or you come back, whichever happens first. Amen.

Reflections and personal notes:_____

_____

_____

_____

_____

_____

_____

_____

_____

_____

IN GAME ANALYSIS - "The Unconditional Prayer of the Utterly Serious"

Photo credit Brian Drake

April 06, 2017 I've had this prayer on the wall of my office throughout all my ministry. It's a prayer I have prayed many times since I got it in 2004. Pastor Jim Andrews wrote it and gave me permission to share it: "The Unconditional Prayer of the Utterly Serious":

"Lord God, my singular ambition in life is to magnify You. I care not what the cost; spend me as you please. On Your arrangements I place no conditions. You set the terms and limits of my service. My only prayer is that You ordain for my life whatever will glorify most Christ through me. If my Savior would be honored more through my death than my life; more in sickness than in health; more in poverty than in wealth; more by the appearance of failure than by the trappings of success; more by anonymity than by notoriety; then your design is my desire. Only let me make a difference!"

Get in the Huddle
April 07, 2017
Success
1 Corinthians 9:25   Every athlete exercises self-control in all things. They do it to receive a perishable wreath, but we an imperishable.

This is true of every successful athlete—strict training. Discipline. The renaissance artist Michelangelo was considered the greatest living artist during his lifetime. He said, "If people knew how hard I worked to get my mastery, it wouldn't seem so wonderful at all."

I resonate with this so deeply. My greatest achievements have happened as a result of hard work.

There are few things we can actually control in life when you think of it. You can't control the trials, the pain, the suffering that comes. But you can control whether you yield to Jesus. I like to tell it to my football players like this: you can control your preparation to know what your job is and understand the game; you can control your effort between the whistles.

Every morning I get up, usually before 6am, grab my prayer shawl, then I pray. This is always after I read my daily devotion by C.H. Spurgeon. Occasionally after the devotion I'll open my bible and just read, or dig deeper into the text covered in the devotion. During every single prayer I pray through the armor of God listed in Ephesians 6:13-17. Then I pray for my family, my men, those who have asked for prayer, wisdom for what to do today, then an affirmation that I want to do His will.

Remember that you aren't competing for an earthly trophy. You're running your race for a prize that will never fade you'll be able to rejoice in it for all of eternity, to the praise of His glory!

God, help me to be disciplined today to follow you; I want to run my race to the praise of Your glory, Amen.

Reflections and personal notes:_____

_____
_____
_____
_____
_____
_____
_____
_____
_____
_____

Get in the Huddle
April 08, 2017
Frontlines
1 Corinthians 9:26   So I do not run aimlessly; I do not box as one beating the air.

Sometimes the grind of the daily routine can seem pointless. Maybe you feel like you're not making a difference by doing your 9-5 or 5-2 or whatever your shift is. It feels like a trap and the grass sure looks greener on that other side.

Let me assure you that being a person of integrity who strives to be the best at their job is not a meaningless pursuit. It honors God. You will never know the impact you've had on someone's life.

In ministry sometimes you hear the phrase, wow, those folks in Africa on the frontlines.

This drives me crazy because the truth is, you and I at home, at work, and at play <u>are</u> on the frontlines too! The battle is all around us, and our enemy is sending wave after wave of attack to the frontlines. You are there and so am I. I will not marginalize the fact that you have to put on the armor of God to stand firm at your job in your daily routine! You turned your eyes away from the temptation on the computer and closed the ad or the browser. You asked a coworker how you could pray for them in the break room, then you stopped and did that right then and there. You noticed a discrepancy in the numbers and reported it, even though it put your job at risk. VICTORY ON THE FRONTLINES! Be faithful in the small things; the purpose in the routine is to honor Jesus by your blameless, relentless work to be the best at what you do.

God, help me to see the purpose in my daily walk, whether it is the ministry of the gospel or the ministry of punching the clock as a faithful employee. Give me the strength to endure what may seem pointless. Amen.

Reflections and personal notes:_____

_____
_____
_____
_____
_____
_____
_____
_____
_____

Get in the Huddle
April 09, 2017
Can't Food God
1 Corinthians 9:27   But I discipline my body and keep it under control, lest after preaching to others I myself should be disqualified.

There are no participation trophies in heaven.

You can't show up to church on Sunday, then act like you're competing during the week. You can't run hard in a race for the first lap, then walk the next 3 and expect to catch up to the competition or win. It doesn't work that way.

You can't hide the truth about your walk with Jesus from God; you can pull the wool over my eyes, but you're not fooling the Lamb of God.

Don't preach one thing with your mouth then not discipline your daily walk with Jesus. It's cheating. You will be disqualified.

Jesus, give me strength to subdue my flesh so that I do not fall into sin. I want to please you today, in your name, amen.

Reflections and personal notes:_____

_____
_____
_____
_____
_____
_____

Get in the Huddle
September 17, 2017
God's Weigh Station
Matthew 11:28-30   Come to me, all who labor and
are heavy laden, and I will give you rest. Take my
yoke upon you, and learn from me, for I am gentle
and lowly in heart, and you will find rest for your
souls. For my yoke is easy, and my burden is light.

When I was driving the kids to school this
morning, the Lord gave me an insight about the
weigh station alongside I-5 south.

Some days it's open and other times it's
closed. I'm not sure how or why that happens, but
when it's open, all the trucks are required to stop and
be weighed before they can continue on the freeway.

God brought to mind the idea that if I'm
burdened His station is always open, unlike this
weigh station! And His weigh station doesn't check
your weight and move you along—it actually
removes your burden and gives you a light yoke to
bear. It doesn't penalize you for having a heavy or
overweight load; instead, you get mercy and the
chance to put your load on Jesus' truck. Also, God's
weigh station doesn't force everyone carrying
burdens to stop. If you want to keep bearing your
burden on your own, God doesn't force you to lay it
down.

Instead, God appeals, through Jesus Christ, to
us to lay our burdens down when we're weary. Are
you tired? Are you overwhelmed by the stuff of life?

Pull off the freeway of life right now to go to God's weigh station!

Father, help me to lay my burdens down; give me rest for all the troubles that are clouding my mind. Amen.

Reflections and personal notes:_____

_____
_____
_____
_____
_____
_____
_____
_____
_____

TIMEOUT – "Not a Victim!"

September 17, 2017 *"Therefore, since we are surrounded by so great a cloud of witnesses, let us also lay aside every weight, and sin which clings so closely, and let us run with endurance the race that is set before us, 2 looking to Jesus, the founder and perfecter of our faith, who for the joy that was set before him endured the cross, despising the shame, and is seated at the right hand of the throne of God."* (Hebrews 12:1-2 ESV)

Today, during my workout, I was feeling pretty bad about myself. It was 6 rounds of:

200M run
12 squats (135#)
6 hang power snatch (135#)
for time

After the 2nd round I wanted to quit so bad. My head was pounding. Chemo week saps my endurance so much, so I kept thinking, 'No one will look down on you for tapping out; you're on chemo. It's ok.' Every time I came to the moment of quit or go on I heard the trainers encouraging me to hang in there. I was watching the other folks working around me.

Another thought kept running through my head immediately after the other one--"I'm not a victim; I can go until I can't go. I managed to finish the 3rd round and I thought, 'There's no way I can finish this whole workout; I'm so tired! It's ok; you're on chemo.' My internal dialogue was something like, 'If you quit now you'll have come this far and left it unfinished. I'm not a victim. I'm not a victim. But I don't have to push thru; if there was an excuse to quit, chemo is pretty ok. Everybody has excuses. This will not be mine. My life will not be defined by my treatment. I'm a child of God. I will have integrity. I will finish! I'M NOT A VICTIM!"

By the time I finished my 4th round I decided to finish, even if I walked. I decided that if I couldn't finish the lifts with good form, I'd drop weight; I'd stay at my weight if I could keep pushing without resting too long.

At the end of the 6th round I pushed hard and let out a couple yells finishing the snatches. I yelled to myself "NOT A VICTIM!" then I dropped the last completed rep on the ground and collapsed on the floor and I shed a couple tears of accomplishment and relief.

I find so much spiritual application in this. Every Christian has the same battle in front of them for Victory in Jesus. We must have faith in God to carry out His work, but we must press into our work.

Maybe the excuses are harsh realities--I can't serve there in missions--my life could be in danger; I can't stand in front of people to talk about Jesus, I get stage fright. The point is, whatever your battle, you are equipped by God to accomplish the work, and you can push through or you can give up.

My physical preparation before chemo week prepared me to push through the day and helped strengthen my foundation of fitness. It's like that in our spiritual lives! God never wastes your experience, training, or time. He is ALWAYS preparing us for what lies ahead.

I praise and thank God for the ability to push through; it's truly a gift from Him. He empowers and energizes my mind and body and my response will not waste HIS work in me. So, let me be spent and used up for God's purpose. I'm thankful for the lesson He taught me today in my workout.

IN GAME ANALYSIS – Link to January 03, 2018 article in The Oregon Faith Report magazine

http://oregonfaithreport.com/2018/01/pastors-terminal-brain-cancer-journey/

Editor JP Luce here - We'll explore more photos and links after the game in chapter six, with links to photos, game footage videos, and video highlights of some of Joel's hits and tackles. Look for number 54 – Go Defense!!

For hyperlinks visit www.calvaryhillpublishing.com

Get in the Huddle
January 26, 2018
Grief
1 Thessalonians 4:13-14 But we do not want you to be uninformed, brothers, about those who are asleep, that you may not grieve as others do who have no hope. For since we believe that Jesus died and rose again, even so, through Jesus, God will bring with him those who have fallen asleep.

In the space of the last 4 weeks, a friend in her 80s passed of cancer and a friend's 6 year old son died of cancer. Both families were believing families. But I noticed a difference in the grief and the pain. In the case of the older gal, she had been fighting cancer a long time and all the preparations for her to be with Jesus were made years in advance of her passing. There was a sense of peace and relief in the family, knowing that mom/grandma was now at rest, finally. In the case of the little boy, there was much more evident pain. Hard questions about God; goodness? Love? Fairness? Faithful? Healer? Powerful?

Matthew 10:37 says, "Whoever loves father or mother more than me is not worthy of me, and whoever loves son or daughter more than me is not worthy of me."

The hard truth is that our grief over the loss of loved ones must not surpass our love and trust in Jesus. Life is a fleeting, fragile gift. The gift of God, however, is eternal life. I've heard it said that grief is love with nowhere to go. And this is somewhat true for the Christian. The object of our love cannot receive it from us. This is so tragic; yet, it is more tragic if it truly has no place to go. This is why we worship the Lord and confess that He gives, and He takes away. This is where our grieving love needs to go, for our own sakes. There is hope in Jesus' Resurrection and this offers a place of rest, a harbor of hope, or a blanket of protection and peace.

Jesus, when I grieve, help me find a place for it to go; bring to mind your attributes; remind me of your great power and love that was expressed to and for me thru Your cross. I love you, amen.

Reflections and personal notes:_____

_____

_____

_____

_____

_____

_____

_____

_____

_____

TIMEOUT – "Prognosis"

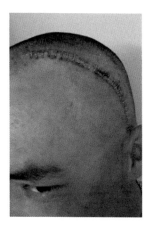

January 26, 2018 Last night I was talking with my wife and the word "prognosis" came up. Honestly, I don't like this word. It's not that I'm in denial of my situation; not at all. I just refuse to trust in the word of man.

They say 2 to 5 years. I don't care about the prognosis. The ONLY word that MATTERS to me is what God says about it. No one can determine my destiny but Him. I trust in His sovereignty, even as others would scoff and say 'you doing the work, Joel.'

Prognosis for my brain resection surgery:
5% death
50% right side paralysis
45% varying levels of symptoms related to nerve damage

Done that. I'm stronger and more fit today than I was last January. The Neurosurgeon was able to remove 95-96% of my tumor.

I asked my doctor how much time I had, worse-case scenario. She said 12 months. 90-95% of my people with this cancer die of it within 5 years.

It's so weird sometimes because I'm like, "I'm going to beat the odds; God is with me." But then other people say the same types of things to me and inside I get angry. Isn't that weird? What about the 95%? That's why I get angry. God was with all the Christians that had glioblastoma and was a comfort for those who sought it even while they weren't believers.

I get angry about the 95% because if I have a long 'DFI' (disease-free-interval) what makes me worth being healed? I'm no better than anyone else with glioblastoma. I'm reminded (and please don't get me wrong here) all the time about just how many people are praying for me.

For whatever reason, the 95% comes back to mind. Surely, I'm not the only Christian to battle this primary cancer and certainly not the first. It is humbling to know that so many care enough to pray for me. But, why not others too? Many people have prayed for those who perished.

Is this guilt I'm carrying? Premature guilt, since I'm barely into my 1st year of glioblastoma?

I think about death more often now and can picture many things that I couldn't imagine before I got sick. What are the things that need to be done before I go?

Don't tell me it's a lack of faith! I absolutely pray to be in that 5%. I've beaten the odds and surpassed every expectation for recovery that I was given to date. Every MRI shows improvement so far. But, how could you tell me it's a lack of faith to realize that 95% is bad odds?

And what's the great fear? I'm going to heaven. Jesus will be there and all those who have gone before me. Isn't this what the Gospel is about?

I believe I will see the goodness of the Lord in the land of the living; and I ask God to let me stay and be a witness to Him and His light; He gets all the glory for my recovery. But this isn't a bargaining chip that brings expectations for God to preserve me past 5 years.

My prayer is to stay for the sake of my bride and children. Gray hair and hip replacements sound alright to me if it means growing old with my love. Having kids, being at their graduation, and walking them down the aisle; having grandkids that I could love and be a blessing and mentor to them; there are the desires of my heart. I want to have a long life, to the praise of God's glory.

I don't want to die, but honestly, everybody does. So, is it that big of a deal?

It's an experience of life, to show that there is so much good and love to be shared. These are the things that matter to me.

IN GAME ANALYSIS

by Leslie Royce

The idea of losing a spouse comes like a sucker punch to the gut. The wind is knocked out of you and the pain lingers in your core. There is an ongoing dull ache constantly reminding you that this news isn't going away anytime soon. It is accompanied by an intermittent sharp stab that prevents you from really catching your breath.

Losing a loved one is hard. Losing a spouse is on a whole different level. Physically it is impossible to live with half a heart. Yet, as a widow that is what you do- you continue to live when half of you is gone.

Maybe you have suspected and attempted to prepare mentally because your spouse is in poor health or makes risky decisions. Or maybe, like me, there was no indication, no sign or symptom. In either circumstance there is no way to soften the blow and a sort of haze takes over. You become preoccupied with questions that have no definitive answers. How will I care for him or her? How will I pay the bills? How can I continue to work, how can I possibly afford not to? How will I manage the kids by myself?

In times like this people say some real stupid things. It's not poetic and it's not helpful but they mean well. I could give you a list of things that people say that are both theologically incorrect and downright rude. It's hard to keep in mind that they are trying to be helpful. One of those phrases that is said a lot is "new normal". I scoffed the first few times it was said to me. "I know you are overwhelmed and hurting right now, but once treatment starts it will soon just be the new normal for you".

"No!" I thought "Joel being sick or dying will never be normal".

I was wrong.

But so were they.

You see, it wasn't that facing the mortality of my spouse became more acceptable over time. It wasn't that I got comfortable with chemotherapy or with waiting for the next MRI or with the idea that I could be a single mom with 7 kids. I found peace in trusting Christ in the face of uncertainty and peace amid chaos; this became my "new normal".

I wish I could describe some wonderful quiet meditative prayer practice that brought me to this place of peace. That is what a "good" pastor's wife would share with you. If I did that, I would be lying. The things that brought me to peace were ugly, gritty, maybe even be shameful. I was angry. To be completely honest, I felt betrayed by God himself. You see, I was widowed before- at the age of 21, with 2 small kids. Was a "good God" really going to leave me widowed again? What in the world would I say to those kids who had already lost a father? How do I look them in the face and tell them that "all things work together for the good of those who love Him?"

When your head is underwater and there is nothing else to grab onto, sometimes you cling to the cross so tightly you get splinters in your hands.

I cried out to God in anger, and he repaid me with peace. I shook my fist at God and called him a betrayer and he repaid me with hope. I cried out because I felt like I was drowning in everything going on around me and he gave me rest. I asked God for a word and he gave me Psalm 57:1 "Be merciful to me, O God, be merciful to me, for in you my soul takes refuge; in the shadow of your wings I will take refuge, till the storms of destruction pass by."

We don't always get the answers that we are looking for. In this earthly life. Sometimes we just don't get answers at all, mountains remain unmoved and sick people sometimes pass away. But God will always give us what we need. If you ask me, we can all use hope, peace and rest.

Agape Photography by Reveena

Agape Photography by Reveena

Get in the Huddle
January 27, 2018
Open to Wisdom
Proverbs 1:26-27 I also will laugh at your calamity;
I will mock when terror strikes you, when terror
strikes you like a storm and your calamity comes like
a whirlwind, when distress and anguish come upon
you.

Wisdom is the one speaking in these verses.
She's pointing out that she called, and the hearer
refused to listen to all her counsel and all her reproof.
So, she'll laugh at the calamity that comes. And I can
hear that laughter when I ignore the way of wisdom.
It's so obvious to me what I should have done after
the fact!

But, wisdom has counsel for this too. Wait on
the Lord and inquire of Him, even if you're not sure
what to do next. There is always a way to find
wisdom. In fact, in the few verses preceding the
laughter, she's recorded as crying out, having cried
aloud in the street, and as calling out to anyone
who'd listen. Wisdom is not too far from a person,
unless they are stubborn and stiff-necked.
Unteachable people reap the whirlwind of calamity
with no comfort save what God gives in the moment.
This is a wonderful and terrible truth.

On the one hand, by not listening to wisdom,
we get ourselves into so many pickles. On the other
hand, by calling out to the Lord, we get ourselves
peace and comfort. And, thankfully, we get a path to
follow thru the terror that has come.

Lord, make me teachable so that I can hear the words of wisdom when they call! I don't want to miss the best way that you have for me, in Jesus' name, amen.

Reflections and personal notes:_____

_____

_____

_____

_____

_____

_____

_____

_____

_____

Get in the Huddle
March 12, 2018
Can't Hide from God
Romans 14:12   So then each of us will give an
account of himself to God.

Bodycams. Police use of force. Sound bites
and clips on youtube. Video on the web is
overwhelming! Anyone with an iPod can make a
video about anything; the editing capabilities of these
are amazing, too. You can do an HD video on a tiny
handheld device, then post it within seconds online
to a potential world-wide audience. Yet, there are
still secrets; still things unseen. Despite all the
visibility everywhere, we humans still are good at
hiding things.

One of my favorite things about game day is
the play by play announcing. It can make or break a
TV broadcast. It makes the game more enjoyable to
hear the call of an announcer rooting hard for your
team! It's a running commentary about what is
happening live in the game.

Well, one day we will give God a full play by
play of every single day of our lives. THINK of it.
You will have the pages of your life storybook
opened, and you will walk God through every single
thing you ever did and said. And, this is before His
judgment seat.

God, thank you for sending your Son, Jesus
Christ. Thank you that in Him, I have forgiveness of
sin. All my sin. Thank you for nailing my sins to the

cross. Accept me according to your promise of eternal life in Jesus. Amen.

Reflections and personal notes:_____

_____
_____
_____
_____
_____
_____
_____
_____
_____

HALFTIME – THE S.O.A.P. METHOD

There comes a point in every grown person's life where there is a transition from baby food to solid food. We need to go beyond the idea of praying everyday and attending a weekly worship service. God is calling each of us not just to be disciples but to disciple others. We are to share the Gospel with others, and when we have people around us that are younger in the faith, we are called to share from the lessons in grace God has given to us in our experience.

To help facilitate this growth, allow me to introduce a method of studying the bible the will help you to be devoted to Jesus every day. It's called, the SOAP method, created by Pastor Wayne Cordeiro of New Hope Church, Honolulu, Hawaii.

---

[2] Isaiah 41, New International Version.

With a bible, journal and a pen in front of you, you pray, asking God for insight—something for you and something for you to share with others. Ask God to teach, correct and encourage you in your faith during your devotional time. Our church, New Hope Legacy, on the Big Island of Hawaii, uses the Life Journal, which has a daily reading program. During your readings you select a passage of scripture that really impacts or stands out from what you read. It could be one verse, or an entire selection.

This is the first step is Scripture, the "S" in SOAP. You write or type the scripture reference in your journal; this can be a single verse, a section of verses, or even a collection of verses from various passages in your reading plan for that day. You just read and underline or make note of any scriptures that stand out to you or that grab your attention. If this doesn't happen, then just pick something to write in your journal.

The next step is Observation. This is the "O" in SOAP. What do you see in the scriptures you're reading? What's happening in the larger context? Make observations about what you're reading. Who is speaking? Is this an old testament promise? Is this something that people deal with today? What insight does this passage give about God, nature, heaven, humanity, etc? Jot these down in your journal.

Next is Application, the "A" in SOAP. You are simply asking, in light of these observations, how will I be affected today? What things in my life will be different? Are there things that need to be different? How can I apply this scripture and observation to my life?

Finally, the last step is Prayer—the "P" in SOAP. This is a written prayer related to your journal entry. Ask God for help to apply it. Pray for whatever is on your heart. Check out https://lifejournal.cc for more information about this approach, resources and journals for purchase.

And there you have it. I'll give you an example of this method from the Psalm that has been the comfort of my heart and soul since I was diagnosed with cancer.

S-Psalm 57:1 "Be merciful to me, O God, be merciful to me, for in you my soul takes refuge; in the shadow of your wings I will take refuge, till the storms of destruction pass by."

O-The psalmist King David cried out to God. The heading of the Psalm indicates that David wrote this while he was hiding in caves when King Saul was chasing him. King Saul intended to kill David. David, outnumbered and hiding in a cave, begged God for mercy. He found refuge in God until the storms of destruction passed by.

A-I cry out to God to have mercy on me for healing; I will take refuge in time with God in prayer, worship, reading the scriptures, and fellowship with the church. The storm of cancer has passed by; I hid my hope and trust in God, not in man. I realize that the rain falls on the righteous and the wicked, but God, in His mercy, has healed me.

P-Lord, be merciful to me; help me to regain feeling in my right side. And whenever the storms rise against me, let me never forget or neglect to take refuge in the shadow of your wings. Amen

This halftime adjustment to do SOAP journaling will be reflected in the second half of this book. These journal entries show my fight to have peace and faith in God. For the purpose of space, only the book, chapter, and verse are referenced. It is my hope that you will open a bible and read the scripture I listed before you read the rest of the SOAP entry.

With this daily SOAP journaling, you will find yourself available to God to mentor someone else! You are feeding yourself and are now able to offer spiritual food to others.

CHAPTER 3 – THIRD QUARTER

July 29, 2018
Steadfast Love
S-Psalm 103:11
O-God's love for me is as high as the heavens. It is an incomprehensibly high heaven. How great is that love? It's not just for me or over me, like an intense feeling. It's toward me. It's extended to me. This makes God's love a personal thing._____

_____

_____

_____

     A-I will live today knowing that God's love is greater than my little fears. OK, they're big, but not as high as the
heavens._____

_____

_____

_____

     P-*Father, thank you for showing me your great love that is higher than the heavens. It is a big love. Massive love. Infinite love. I'm overwhelmed that you could love someone like me, let alone that much. Help me receive your love; let me be overwhelmed by How Great and How Much it is. Amen*

July 30, 2018
I Saw You
S-John 1:48-49

O-Jesus has knowledge about us without being bodily around. He is the Son of God, according to first chapter in the gospel of John, and this is one of the signs. Jesus called Nathaniel out for being a real Israelite, without deceit. Jesus knows because He is God's son.

A-Jesus knows me. He knows my heart, my desires, my fears, and my hopes. I ask, "How do you know me?" He sees me, not just in the physical sense. He loves me, yet, still.

P-Heavenly Father, thank you for not leaving me alone. Thank you that you see me and love me yet still. Amen

July 31, 2018
God of Action
S-Isaiah 64:4
O-People who wait on God have him act on their behalf. God acts. People wait for Him.

_____

_____

_____

A-This is hard, but this scripture reminds me that God will show up. If I wait on Him, then He will act. God is patiently waiting to see if I will wait and not run ahead of His will.

_____

_____

_____

P-*Heavenly Father, help me to wait on you! I can't do anything without you. Shape me and mold me, for you are the Potter and I am the clay.*

August 1, 2018
God Hears
S-Isaiah 65:24; John 3:33-36
O-God knows what's on my mind before I speak a word. He hears me. Jesus' testimony about Himself and the Father is true. The Father put Jesus in charge of everything. You have to obey Jesus to get eternal life. Believers have eternal life. God's wrath is on anyone who doesn't believe in Jesus.

_____

_____

_____

A-I am reminded to put my trust in Jesus. I want to be found with eternal life when I die. God hears and knows what is in my heart before I ever consider what's within and what my thoughts and emotions are. Utter vulnerability before God, yet He hears me.

_____

_____

_____

P-*Father, thank you that you hear me. Before I say a word you know my thoughts, fears, doubts, hopes, dreams, visions, etc. Thank you for giving me eternal life. Thank you for real hope. Please bring back a clear scan. Help me be faithful. Show me how to love my wife* and *children today. I ask for wisdom* and *discernment about NHL Reach. What if anything do I/we do? Leave? Stay? Help Lord. Please grant me victory over anxiety* and *fear. I want to follow you* and *not hold back. Amen*

August 2, 2018
Offer Sacrifices
S-2 Chronicles 33:16
O-Manasseh restored worship, made peace
with God and showed gratitude.

A-The way to overcome defeat is to
continually restore the altars of prayer and worship.
I'm to show gratitude for God's deliverance.

P-*Father, thank you so much for my healing.
Forgive my unbelief. I worship you, the God who
hears!*

August 3, 2018
Take Refuge
S-Nahum 1:7
O-God is good. God's a stronghold when trouble comes. He knows everyone who take refuge in him! Only those who know him can take refuge.

_____

_____

A-I will take refuge in God when trouble comes.

_____

_____

P-*Father, help me, remind me, encourage me to take refuge in you! You are my hope* and *peace. Amen*

August 4, 2018
The Bread Test
S-John 6:5,29,44

O-Jesus tests his disciples to see whether they believe he can provide. Jesus is the bread. He's the limitless supply. God's work is to believe in Jesus, whom He sent. God draws people to Himself. Jesus raises the dead.

_____
_____
_____
_____
_____
_____

A-I'm reminded to believe in the resurrection. I must trust Jesus is God's bread. My job is to tell the message. My programming or service is not what draws people to Jesus. You can draw a crowd with food, entertainment and so on, but the Father draws hearts. I need only share about Jesus being sent to save us. I will use words because it is necessary. Faith comes by hearing.

_____
_____
_____

P-*Heavenly Father, I believe you sent your son to save the world. He is the only true bread. Thank you for drawing me to you. Thank you in advance for a clear MRI. Thank you for my mom being here. Amen*

August 5, 2018
Heart Water
S-John 7:37-39

O-Jesus was not quiet in declaring Himself the source of eternal life. Anyone can come to Jesus. Out of the hearts of believers will flow living water, the message of the gospel to others.

_____

A-I must not be quiet about what Jesus has done in and thru me! I'm saved once, but filled many many times with the Holy Spirit. And again, the purpose is to introduce others to Jesus.

_____

P-*Heavenly Father, fill me with your Holy Spirit. Bring opportunities to shine your light. I'm thirsty for you. Amen*

August 6, 2018
Bear Witness
S-John 8:24,28,31,34-36
O-Without believing in Jesus everyone will die in their sins. Jesus proved Himself on the cross because that was His obedience. He did the Father's will. True disciples abide in Jesus' word. In other words, they spend time in the scriptures. The truth will set true disciples free! People who practice sin are slaves. The son is in the house permanently; slaves are temporary in the house. The son can free the slaves so they can remain in the house.

_____

_____

_____

A-I'm not longer a slave to sin. I have been set free! When I saw the Son of Man lifted up, I believed what he said, "I am he." I repent of not believing I've been set free.

_____

_____

_____

P-*Help me remember* and *know that I have been set free from the shackles of sin* and *the bondage of fear. You conquered the grave. I repent of my unbelief* and *give you praise, glory* and *honor. Amen* `

August 7, 2018
Quieted by Love
S-Zephaniah 3:17a; John 9:37
O-God quiets not by sushing but by love. The response to Jesus was personal, public worship. The healed man believed.

_____
_____
_____

A-I must accept God's love; I've been quieted by His love. I have to remember to worship Jesus because I believe in Him, not because He healed me.

_____
_____
_____

P-*Father, help me accept your love. I'm scared and anxious. But you are my God and savior. I will worship you, my savior and Lord, Jesus Christ.*

August 8, 2018
God Sends and Delivers
S-Jeremiah 1:7-8,17
    O-If you are obeying God, it doesn't matter
how old you are. If God calls you to share, then age
is not the issue; obedience is. Don't be afraid of
opposition. God, in His work, in His will, will
deliver you. If one disobeys then public knowledge
of your fear is given.

_____

_____

_____

_____

_____

    A-I'm reminded how God called me to
ministry as a youth but I rejected the call until I was
21. I dress/prepare myself to minister and serve
Jesus.

_____

_____

_____

_____

_____

    P-*Heavenly Father, teach me how to be
brave. Help me to have courage to do your will.
Amen*

August 9, 2018
The Resurrection
S-John 11:3-4,32b-33,51

O-Jesus loved Lazarus. He knew the outcome before it happened. Jesus was deeply moved and troubled in their grief of loss. They believed if only he'd been there their brother wouldn't have died. They trusted in Jesus in his presence. The high priest prophesied what would happen and this spurred the Jewish leaders to plan Jesus' death.

_____

_____

A-Jesus loves me -"No greater love..." I recall the loss of my brother and think, Lord, if you'd been there my brother wouldn't have died. Sufficient enough is faith in the resurrection on the last day. What a day of rejoicing that WILL be! My heart is moved at how Jesus loves and what motivates Him. He wants to give eternal life. He wants to take care of me. He can comfort me because he experienced the emotional trauma of death and loss. The high priest serves as an example to me to slow down and discern God's will. The Jewish leaders misinterpreted that prophesy. They thought it applied to them, and their position. They got it wrong. I must wait on the Lord, and get it right.

_____

_____

_____

P-*Heavenly Father, you have saved me. You are the resurrection* and *the life! I love how you love me. So completely* and *I'm undone. I'm in awe that you love me like Lazarus; you weep when I weep* and *hurt when I hurt. I pick up on the anger over death* and *how motivated you were/are to beat death! Thank you for the promise not to take me from Leslie. Lead me* and *help me* and *guide me to love her in light of your mercy towards me. Thank you for the prophecy from Irene through the chapter 11 in the gospel of John. Amen*

August 10, 2018
When the End Comes
S-Jeremiah 5:20-21; John 12:19,27,42
O-The leaders in Jeremiah's day were false
and led people astray. They got status, position but
God asked What about when the ends comes? Game
Over. The Pharisees rightly observed but wrongly
applied the truth about the people coming to Him.
They were upset that they gained nothing. Jesus was
incredibly troubled but He didn't let it stop His
mission. "I come for this; should I ask God to take it
away? No; this is why I came to earth." The
authorities feared man whereas Jesus feared God.
They believed not, and let their fear keep them from
God. They loved glory from man more than that
from God. Jesus was passionate about his message.
He declared that the Father's commandment to Jesus
was eternal life—that when he obeyed it would offer
salvation to everyone who believed in him.

_____

_____

A-This is a warning not to love the glory
from man. I must make regular checks to determine
if I'm seeking God's glory or my glory. Personal gain
means nothing in God's economy. Jesus didn't let his
fear stop him from obeying God and neither should I.
So, today? What is your will for me? I believe that
you, Jesus are eternal life.

_____

_____

_____

_____

_____

_____

P-*Father, give me strength* and *courage like Jesus, to serve in spite of a troubled heart. To love* and *live life! Amen*

CHALLENGE FLAG! – The Bible is from God vs "The Bible is full of contradictions."

 *stock photo*

We need to acknowledge and deal with objections to our faith. There needs to be conversations about these. Why does it appear that there are contradictions in the Bible?

For the purposes of this challenge flag, we are going to look at some "contradictions" in the Bible:

- How did Judas Iscariot die? Was it by hanging or falling headlong?
- Did Jesus bear his own cross or did Simon of Cyrene?
- How many demoniacs met Jesus at Gerasene?

When you are studying and working thru these apparent contradictions keep in mind that a contradiction on occurs if one statement makes the other impossible and both are supposed to be true. If

I say, "I love you" and "I hate you," this is an explicit contradiction. But if I said, "I have a love/hate relationship with you," it means that I love some things about you and hate some things about you. This is called an apparent contradiction.

The gospel of Matthew records that Judas died by hanging. The Acts of the Apostles says he fell and his bowels gushed out. These are both true. We can infer that he hung himself and then after a time the rope, or the branch, broke and his bowels burst open in the decomposition process.

The gospel of John records that Jesus bore his own cross to Golgotha, and the other three gospels record that Simon bore it. There is no contradiction; John 19:17 doesn't say Jesus bore His cross alone. Considering the physical trauma Jesus had just gone thru, it would be understandable that the soldiers would grab a passer-by to assist Jesus in carrying the cross.

The gospel of Matthew records 2 demon possessed men came out to meet Jesus in Gerasene. The gospel of Mark and Luke record that a man met Jesus in Gerasene. This is an apparent contradiction, but Mark and Luke don't say only one man came to Jesus there.

It would be like me telling of a prayer meeting I attended while I was going through chemo treatments. A man prayed for me to be healed of cancer. If you asked the other leaders, they would tell you that two men prayed for me to be healed of cancer. I didn't contradict them; I just didn't mention that there were two that prayed for me. One is memorable to me, because he was shouting his prayer into my ear.

So, when I recall the event, I remember, this one man prayed for my healing very intensely. And it is also true that two men prayed for my healing, as well as a woman, in Ebenezer's Coffeehouse in Washington D.C. that evening!

I would commend two web resources to you for further study and research: Christian Apologetics and Research Ministry (www.carm.org), and Answers in Genesis (www.answersingenesis.org).

August 11, 2018
Washed by Jesus
S-John 13:8b,10,34-35,44a,50
O-Without being washed by Jesus, there is no share in eternal life or resurrection to life. Jesus provided an example for believers. He humbled Himself. He gave a new commandment to love one another.

_____
_____
_____
_____
_____

A-I must be washed by the blood of the lamb. I must serve in humility my brothers and sisters in Christ. What are the things beyond foot washing that are needed? To serve in humbleness and love? To love requires humility because we give up the idea that we're better than someone else, and foot washing is needed. The world won't know that I'm a disciple unless/until I love my brothers and sisters in Christ.

_____
_____

P-*Father, teach me to love when I'm offended, when I'm scared, when I'm angry—truly to be humble. Amen*

September 7, 2018
Salvation Has Come
S-Revelation 12:10

O-The accuser is thrown down. Salvation has come in Jesus. Power has come in Jesus. The kingdom of God has come with Jesus. Jesus has the authority-to save, to give power, to advance the kingdom, and to overcome the accuser. Jesus threw the devil down! The devil can't accuse me in any way that sticks any longer.

_____

_____

A-I've been spared, saved, and covered by Jesus! I'm reminded of who I am – not what I've done or who I've been! The accuser is thrown down in my life!

_____

_____

P-*Father, help me not remember the accusations against me. The devil has been thrown down* and *what he meant for evil you brought so much good.*

September 8, 2018
Next Gen
S-Psalms 48:13-14; Revelation 13:10
    O-The older are to communicate to the next generation who God is; what His kingdom is like; and how He guides and will guide us forever. Persecution will come to the saints through captivity or martyrdom. Christians are to endure and to keep the faith.

———————————————————————
———————————————————————
———————————————————————
———————————————————————
———————————————————————
———————————————————————

    A-It is my task to teach my children who God is, to tell how He has guided me and show them His great works. I'm also to endure suffering and any persecution that comes on account of my faith in God's Christ!

———————————————————————
———————————————————————
———————————————————————

    P-*Heavenly Father, I have need of deliverance* and *strength to prepare for worship* and *make ready my children. I have started dipping with stress. Clean me, change my heart* and *mind about what I need. And that's more of you! Amen*

September 9, 2018
Fear and Glorify God
S-Revelation 14:7,12-13

O-People are to fear God and give Him glory. Why? Because the judgment of who is and isn't righteous has come (faith in Jesus) and because He is the creator of heaven and earth, the sea and the springs of water. God MADE it all. Nothing evolved. The saints must have endurance to walk with Jesus! Those who claim His name and keep His commands (i.e. love one another, forgive one another, serve one another) must have endurance to continue in those ways! Deeds of the saints in life follow into death - and it is blessed to die in the Lord!

_____
_____

_____

A-I must remember not to lose heart, especially about my circumstance. I must fear God and give Him glory! The righteous deeds I've done in this life will follow me into the next one that is in the Lord's presence. Absent from the body, present with the Lord. And whatever I lack in fine linens (righteous deeds), Jesus makes it full and complete.

_____
_____

_____

P-*Father, give me more faith* and *grace to believe in your healing* and *in your work in my life* and *that of my family. Show me, guide me* and *I will follow. I praise* and *glorify you! Amen*

117

September 10, 2018
God Never Fails
S-Lamentations 3:22-26
O-God's love never, never, stops; it never fails. Waiting on the Lord is a good plan!

_____

_____

_____

_____

_____

_____

A-I will wait quietly for God. I trust His love and mercy won't fail me.

_____

_____

_____

_____

_____

P-*Lord, help me remember you first every day. You really are my portion* and *my hope. I couldn't face my life, let alone my death, without you!*

118

September 11, 2018
God is True
S-Revelation 16:7
O-God Almighty is true! He is wholly just!
This scripture is in the middle of God's wrath being
poured out.

_____
_____
_____
_____
_____

A-This is a solemn reminder to share the
Gospel with others. It's a reminder to love others and
have compassion on them. I know their fate.

_____
_____
_____
_____
_____

P-*God, give me your heart for people. Also,
let me teach myself before I teach others! Amen*

September 12, 2018
Lamb Chops!
S-Revelation 17:14
O-The Lamb conquers all God's enemies!
Everybody set up against Jesus is conquered.

_____

A-Jesus is battling with my flesh and He will
have final victory. He is victorious in every battle.
I'm called and chosen and faithful.

_____

P-*Father, clean my heart, oh God! Amen*

September 13, 2018
God's Pleasure
S-Ezekiel 33:11
O-God's pleasure is that of the wicked turning from their evil ways! This is the appeal of the gospel.

_____

_____

_____

A-This is a check to my attitude about people who don't know God. There should be no feelings of pleasure or satisfaction in their deaths. Even enemies

_____

_____

_____.

P-*Father, give me a heart of compassion that pleasures in what you pleasure! I am scared over these symptoms that vary* and *never go away.*

Can't I trust You? Will you keep your promise to heal and *not take another husband away? Prepare me, Lord, to lead and minister. Amen*

September 14, 2018
Do the Deeds
S-Revelation 19:6-9,10d

O-Multitudes worship God because of Christ and the church. The Bride prepares herself by putting on the linens provided to her by the Lamb. God's words are true and the spirit of prophecy is found in the testimony of Jesus!

A-Words of prophecy, by the testimony of Jesus. "I won't take another husband from you." "This doesn't end in death." "Not this one. This one is healed by the blood." "Cancer will not take this one." "You'll see grandchildren." "Your work isn't finished." "Books will be written about me." I'm reminded to do the deeds Jesus has prepared for me to do.

P-*I will* and *do believe your words in the scripture* and *thru the Bride—you prepared her work of prophecy to me before there was time. I'm humbled* and *overwhelmed by your loving care toward me!*

September 17, 2018
Trustworthy and True
S-Revelation 22:6-7

O-The book of Revelation is trustworthy and true. God sends his messenger to show his people what must take place! Jesus is coming soon!

_____

_____

_____

A-I'm convinced that God has spoken in Revelation and to me thru his prophets. He is the God of the spirits of the prophets. They are subject to his true and faithful words! I'm healed of cancer to the praise of His glory for further work in, for, and of the kingdom.

_____

_____

_____

P-*God, help me to keep the words of your book! I want to be blessed. Holy Spirit, lead me and guide me. I trust in You. It doesn't matter what the scan says. Your words CAN'T BE BROKEN. I love you Lord. Amen*

September 18, 2018
How, God?
S-Ezekiel 45:10; Luke 1:15b,45
O-The leaders were to be just and fair in Israel, with balanced scales. John was not to drink alcohol all his days, as only for the Lord—but Zechariah didn't believe and was stricken. Contrast with Mary who believed. It's interesting – Zechariah knew what he had to do – but Mary, she was like, um, How? He gave excuses as to why not, she wondered how it would happen.

_____

_____

_____

A-I'm to be just and fair. Instead of telling God why his Word won't work, I need to wonder at things, how will they work.

_____

_____

_____

P-*Help me, Father, have faith in trust in your word. May Leslie* and *I be counted blessed for believing in the fulfillment of the spirits of the prophets. Amen*

CHAPTER 4 – FOURTH QUARTER

September 19, 2018
Simeon Speaks
S-Luke 2:29-32
O-Simeon was promised by God that he would see the Messiah before he died. God faithfully fulfilled His word to Simeon! He saw the salvation of the Jews and the Gentiles!

A-I have to remember that God brought the light of revelation to the Gentiles. He did this, and kept His word to Simeon. He will keep his word to Leslie. He will keep His word to Irene. He will keep His word to me that He will heal me for the spirit of the prophets is subject to the prophets! And He is the God of the spirits of the prophets.

_____

_____

P-Father, I'm scared and concerned. Yet I trust in You! I fully expect a clear and stable MRI on Monday. You're faithful and true. By the power and blood of Jesus my brain will be stable! What you declare cannot be overturned. You are my hope and peace. Amen.

September 20, 2018
Operation: Enduring Kingdom
S-Daniel 6:26b-27

O-God showed King Darius whose kingdom endured and caused the king of the known world to declare His praise!

_____
_____
_____
_____
_____

A-I will praise the One whose kingdom endures forever!

_____
_____

P-*Inspire me to praise you! I love you, Lord! Amen*

September 21, 2018
Temptation Comes
S-Luke 4:13
O-Jesus resisted the devil and the devil left. The devil waited for an opportune time to tempt, attack, and undermine Jesus.

_____
_____
_____

A-The devil waits for opportune times to tempt – when you're tired, hungry, thirsty, lonely, etc.

_____
_____
_____
_____
_____
_____

P-*God, help me always be ready to resist the devil!*

September 22, 2018
Desolate Prayer
S-Luke 5:16
O-Jesus stayed in the power of God thru prayer. He would be alone to pray and spent much time in prayer.

_____
_____
_____
_____
_____

A-Jesus' example to me is amazing. I'm challenged and reminded to prayer often and fervently.

_____
_____
_____
_____
_____

P-*Heavenly Father, remind me to pray.*

September 23, 2018
Mr. Log-Eye
S-Luke 6:42d

<u>With that, I want to introduce you to Mr. Log-Eye.</u>
There once was a man who walked around,
Pointing out every evil sin that he found.

A student of the bible, he knew the truth,
But on matters of love & reproof he was uncouth.

That he pointed out sin wasn't a big deal,
For as I said, truth is really real.

This man, however, was a hypocrite—
Cuz living in his own sin, he didn't quit!

He'd go around looking for the tiniest speck,
In someone's eye, making others a wreck.

They'd see it though, just as plain as a dog,
That there in his eye was a giant log.

He'd walk around in a big straw hat,
Swinging his head around like a big ol' bat.

The name of this man was Mr. Log-Eye
When you spoke to him, he'd just reply,
"You have a small speck in your eye!
If my name ain't Mr. Log-Eye!"

Every once in a while he would see his error,
Then he'd look at himself, as if with a care.

But the pride & arrogance in his heart,
Caused many a friend & himself, to up & depart

How could anyone listen to this hypocrite?
When looking at his own sin couldn't quit?

The truth is that he really couldn't see,
--I'm speaking to you truthfully--
Through the log in his eye to see clearly
So that he could love people truly & dearly.

Jesus said examine yourself & take the log-eye out;
Then you'll see clearly without any doubt,

Loving others means not judging or condemning
But accepting, sharing & truly forgiving!

So thank you for spending time listening to this tale
About a man who walked this life's long trail

You've been given fair warning now, you see,
If ever a man walks by whose eye holds a tree

Just politely nod & pray for him,
For his head is just caught in a limb,

Ask if he has examined himself, just like you & I
So that he too can be free from the man Mr. Log-Eye

--Joel

O-Hypocrites have logs in their eyes. You can't see clearly to deal with someone else's issue until you deal with yours.

_____

_____

A-I must not be Mr. Log-Eye!

_____

_____

P-*God, what is my log? Bitterness? Anger over offense? I repent* and *ask for forgiveness. Amen*

September 24, 2018
Go in Peace (MRI Day)
S-Psalms 84:11; Luke 7:50

O-God gives favor, honor and good things to those who walk uprightly. Faith in Jesus brings salvation. Saved people can go in peace.

_____

_____

_____

_____

_____

A-I have been given favor of healing, honor of blessing and peace in salvation. God gives me light and protects me.

_____

_____

_____

_____

_____

P-*Father, help me to walk in integrity. I have strongholds* and *lack the effort to manage money. I have no job but I'm too busy? Nay! I am being lazy* and *afraid: more afraid than lazy. Lord help me to do your will. Amen*

September 25, 2018
Faith for Healing (Stable MRI News!)
S-Luke 8:46,48
O-Jesus healed someone unawares! This shows His humanity. It shows that communication is important and necessary with Jesus, not that He doesn't know, but that He is interested in the individual. Faith unlocks/unleashes the healing power of Jesus – not that we have control, but that we'd have humility to say, I'll not bother the Master, but only touch His robe and I'll be healed. She trembled before Him - and He came to set captives of all kinds free.

_____
_____

_____
A-I'll never understand His choices—Harold, April, Ron, Matt, me etc. But He will heal whom He will. I say to myself – if only I can touch your robe I'll be healed.

_____
_____

_____
P-*Jesus, help me – I believe You. Help me overcome my unbelief. Thank You for a second chance at ministry. I know what I need to do. Give me courage to face it.*

September 26, 2018
Arrows
S-Psalms 127:3-4
O-Kids are a good thing! They are fruit and
weapons.

_____

_____

A-Kids can turn rotten and used to hurt
others. The lesson is to raise them in the knowledge
of God and to point them in the right direction.

_____

_____

_____

_____

_____

P-*Father, give me wisdom in directing* and
pointing my arrows!

PENALTY FLAG – PORNOGRAPHY

Personal Foul

stock photo

Pornography. This is a personal foul. A game changing, a game losing, flag. The statistics are mind-boggling.

I was introduced to pornography by HBO as a kid. This introduction led to an on again off again diet of magazines, films, and such during my teenage and early college years. After I gave my heart fully to Jesus, I struggled with the temptation to look at porn. It wasn't until I arrived at seminary that I finally had victory over it, two years after coming to Christ, and one year after being married. I had to learn how to find strength to overcome it; this came through the Holy Spirit. Relying on Him, trusting in His resurrection, and learning to ask the way out from temptation has given me freedom from lust since the summer of 2004.

The worst part of my addiction to pornography, and there were many bad parts, was that I brought that into the first year of my marriage. Our first year of marriage was a hard experience. I tried very hard to break free in my own strength. Even before we got married. When I gave my heart to the Lord, I got rid of everything I had that was even remotely sensual. And I had success in fighting it. But there would be occasional slips.

 Looking back, though, I can see that there was a difference between my response to using porn. Before Christ, I had no remorse; no regret; and I only wanted more of it. After Christ, I felt the guilt of conviction and shame for polluting my body and mind with it. Instead of ongoing acceptance and use of it, it became more of a lapse one day, then a recommitment to leave it behind; then I would go a month, or three weeks, and then lapse again. I think the longest I held out was two months.

It wasn't until I accepted that I needed the power of the Holy Spirit to beat it that I beat it. I remember telling the Lord, God, I can't do this; please help me. Show me a way out to stand up under this.

And that is when I discovered an ad for https://xxxchurch.com. It was either the first or second week of seminary, and I established email accountability for web browsing through this ministry's filter and tracking software. This isn't a fix or cure for your addiction though. You have to desire to please God more than yourself. You must be willing to take the necessary steps to get clean.

If you have been tempted with porn, and but haven't used it, especially if you're a man, don't do it! The man brain is wired in such a way that it will remember the images, forever. It has been nearly 30 years and I can still remember the very first visual I had of pornography. As if it happened yesterday. Even as I type this I am contending and fighting to take every thought captive to Christ! But I have peace and security in Christ. And I have victory! I am unashamed. Because the Gospel of Jesus Christ is the power of God to salvation for everyone who believes!

Leslie, my wife, and I, share open communication now. It's a vulnerable thing to share with your spouse your temptations and struggles. But, I'd rather she know what's happening with me than to hide it from her and then destroy her heart and trust by her finding out. If she knows how I'm struggling, then she'll know how to pray for me. She can help me and remind me to find my identity and Christ. And she can meet that need for sexual pleasure that is healthy and godly in the bounds of marriage!

A resource for parents online can be found at Enough is Enough (www.enough.org).

September 27, 2018
Get to Work
S-Haggai 2:4c; Luke 10:16,20,22
O-God called out Israel to be strong and to work! God is in His works, especially the church. A rejection of Jesus, even a Christian sharing the gospel, is a rejection of God the Father. The rejoicing isn't in God's gifts and delegated authority, rather it is being written in the book of life. Jesus decides who knows God. Many people are deceived thinking they know God when in truth they don't at all. People have an awareness of Him and His attributes thru Creation, but only Jesus reveals the Father to humanity.

A-I have to be strong and get to work! I don't reject Jesus and rejoice in my citizenship in Heaven. I ask for healing and at times lose track of where my true rejoicing and praise comes from. May I not be deceived into false views about God!

P-*Father, thank you for eternal life. Thank you for healing. Keep me in your love* and *will. Forgive me for not being totally up front with Leslie today. Amen*

September 28, 2018
Holy Spirit: The Greatest Gift
S-Luke 11:13,23

O-Evil people can know how to be good
parents – or at least are able to give good gifts. What
a contrast with the father in Heaven. He offers the
Holy Spirit – above every other gift. That's amazing.
I gather most people don't live as if the Holy Spirit
was the best or greatest gift. Jesus draws a hard line
in the proverbial sand – if you're not with Him,
You're against Him. I wonder if the person who
doesn't gather scatters others or themselves? Don't
Gather, You Scatter. He's gathering – souls? Good
works – healing – deliverance from demonic
strongholds.

_____

_____

A-I must be consistent in praying to be filled
with the Holy Spirit and need to learn how to gather!

_____

_____

P-*Father, help me know my next ministry
step. Thank you for Lyle. Thank you for paddling!!
Amen*

September 29, 2018
By the Spirit
S-Zechariah 4:6; Luke 12:3
O-It's not by the power and strength of people that there is victory! It's by the wonderful and good gift of the Holy Spirit! There are no secrets and everything hidden will be revealed. God's Spirit will do this.

A-The Holy Spirit is my gift. The given one. The shared one. I must guard my mouth and the words I speak in the dark and in the hidden places.

P-*Father, fill me with your Holy Spirit. Teach me to repent* and *confess. Teach me to forgive. You are the Creator* and *God of the universe. I praise You! Amen*

September 30, 2018
Unlooked for Healing
S-Luke 13:11-13

O-This woman didn't seek out Jesus. He saw her and was about to teach a lesson about and on the Sabbath Day. He called her disability a work of Satan. He has power to disable people, but Jesus called her. She was healed, even as Jesus was unlooked for!

A- Jesus notices and cares about people with disability, including me. Jesus, are you telling me to take Keppra?

P-*Father, thank you for the repeated good report about my scan. All the symptoms occurred with NO CHANGE in the scan. Lessons, Father! Thank you. Amen*

October 1, 2018
Done Great Things
S-Psalms 126:1-3
O-When God restores us people dream.
Laughter and shouts of joy come with deliverance.
People say, God has done great things for them.

_____
_____
_____

A-God HAS done great things for me and my
family. Forgiveness, not holding my, Leslie's, or the
kids' sins against us. Others say, regularly, God has
done great things for us.

_____
_____
_____

P-*Help me never forget where my help comes
from* and *how you have done it. I'm healed and
delivered from cancer. Amen*

October 2, 2018
God's Promise
S-Psalms 147:10-11
O-God's not impressed by my army, my strength etc. He takes pleasure in people who trust in Him and not the creation.

_____

_____

_____

_____

_____

A-I want to be someone God takes pleasure in!

_____

_____

_____

_____

_____

P-*Father, take me* and *make me pleasurable to you! I HOPE IN YOUR LOVE!!! Amen*

October 3, 2018
Preservation
S-Psalms 138:7; Luke 16:10-11
O-God preserves people in trouble, He finds dishonest people dishonest; he finds honest people honest.

_____

_____

A-Lord, let it not be me you deliver from trouble for dishonesty. Give me courage to manage as you will!

_____

_____

P-*Father...I keep coming* and *saying the same prayers. I haven't made a change in tracking. I've never been long-term faithful in that. What do I need to do? Thank you for deliverance in trouble. Amen*

October 8, 2018
The Weaned
S-Psalms 131:2

O-A weaned child is comforted and quieted in her arms. Satisfied. Stilled. How many souls are not weaned or at rest with God? Troubled hearts—crying babes—not to jeer, but to sympathize and pity. How great is the peace of one weaned in their soul!

A-I must learn to quiet my heart and soul before the LORD—reminds one of the song. I'll let my words be few – Jesus I am so in awe of you.

P-*Lord, thank you for peace—thank you for rest. I pray for strength* and *courage* and *I wait on you. This AWANA deal? This Ohana group? This rental? Amen.*

October 9, 2018
Dwell in Unity
S-Nehemiah 1:5; Psalms 133:1
O-God is faithful to those who love Him—He is steadfast. He's unmovable, unshakeable. Mighty. Brothers dwelling in unity is a beautiful thing. Needs are anticipated, problems are dwelt with together, there's joy, laughter and a "flow" to conversation and work.

_____
_____
_____

A-I must take steps to show that I love God and desire His will and purpose. Am I a brother that dwells peacefully or peaceably? Or do I bring disunity?

_____
_____
_____

P-*Help me, God, be a bringer of unity! Amen*

October 10, 2018
Taunt Turns
S-Nehemiah 4:4

O-Longing for justice knows no singular culture. Something inside of people wants justice and vindication. The Israelites were doing what God called them to and were taunted for it. It's a prayer for the oppressed but I'm reminded of the prayers of the martyrs—forgive them!

_____
_____
_____
_____
_____
_____

A-My enemies are God's enemies, only by His choice and grace. It is ok to pray for justice, but I think it's better to appeal to God for mercy.

_____
_____
_____

P-*Father, let me have a revealed response to my enemies rather than vengeful thinking. But, if I don't feel the push to share mercy, but the need for justice, let me pray like these faithful builders. You vindicate me; you turn back the taunts, Amen.*

October 14, 2018
The Author
S-Psalms 1:3; Acts 3:15
O-The righteous are solid yet flexible. Flexible but not swayed from roots. Timing matters in fruit bearing? There is blessing and anointing in the life of the follower of Jesus. Jesus is the Author!

The Author of Life. The Apostles Peter and John only claimed to be witnesses of resurrection and conduits of the power of His resurrection by faith! Perfect health, by faith.

_____
_____
_____

A-I've been healed, by faith. I'm watered by Jesus' living water and I'm ready to produce fruit!

_____
_____
_____
_____
_____

P-*Father, use me as you will to be a witness. Give me power* and *favor to witness to your healing resurrection truth* and *power. Amen*

October 15, 2018
Builders
S-Acts 4:11,14

O-The people of God are the builders! More than that, the stones. We bring more stones by sharing the gospel! Nobody can deny the evident work of God! My healing—my testimony can't be denied! I didn't get peace, strength and courage from vibes or the Universe. God spoke to Leslie and me through His people and they have proved right and true!

_____
_____
_____

A-I'm a builder! And I have a testimony you can't oppose.

_____
_____
_____
_____
_____

P-*Father, I want to be a builder in your temple! Use me. AWANA clubs? Lord, help. Amen. Thank you for peace.*

October 16, 2018
Distinction
S-Malachi 3:18
O-God treats His people with goodness. All things work together for good to those who love Him! And His wrath is on unbelievers. His people must wait for His vindication and deliverance.

_____
_____
_____
_____
_____
_____

A-I am a recipient of preferential treatment!

_____
_____
_____
_____
_____

P-*Thank you father, for showing me the blessing of being your child. Amen*

IN GAME ANALYSIS – "Grief, Hope and Peace, Leveling the Playing Field"

by Dale Royce (Joel's dad)

November 21, 2018

On Easter Monday some years ago my mother called to tell me that my father had passed away in the night. He was a young 67 years old. He was my confidant and friend; not just my father. I felt so much loss and grief and my soul felt a hollow emptiness. He was a veteran of three military campaigns and there were so many questions I wanted more answers to. I wanted back all of those moments I had with him.

Only nine years earlier my older sister Sandie had passed away, and now my own father at such a young age. I felt so much loss and grief. My soul needed healing.

Although I preached dad's funeral, I don't even remember what was said, except I thought I did a terrible job. Dad's death and a rocky marriage led me to a depression lasting several months. I wondered if life was even worth living. It was in this dark place that I remembered a theme from chorus, "Because He lives, I can face tomorrow…and life is worth the living just because He lives".

I was reminded that Jesus will always provide hope in the darkness of despair and grief. When I was so faithless and hanging on to grief, Jesus remained faithful, hanging on to me. God came to my rescue. He strengthened me, renewed me and comforted me. His strength and hope are what I depend upon. What I didn't know then was that God was preparing me for a fiery trial I would experience ten years later, in 2002.

I was a bi-vocational pastor in Hood River and chaplain at the Oregon Veteran's Home. My secular job was in Portland. On the morning of November 4th when driving to work, I noticed first responders tending to an automobile crash on the access road. It never dawned on me that it would involve me in the most terrible way.

That morning my wife Glenda came to work with the horrible news that our nineteen year old son Anthony had died in the automobile crash I had driven by that morning. The laws of physics and speed in a small vehicle were too much for him to overcome.

I was devastated beyond words. I understood how it could happen, but struggled with why it happened. Anthony was the prodigal son who came home. He was recently employed and was just beginning to discover who he was in this world. I made a brave face, but inwardly was inconsolable. I was hurt and angry and deeply bruised in my soul. There was no one to blame. It was an accident that didn't need to happen.

During this time of intense grief I was reminded of when King David fasted for the life of his infant son, who later passed away. When asked why he stopped fasting in his grief his reply was (paraphrased) that although he can not return to me, I will one day return to him. The Bible is a consistent witness throughout that Jesus Christ is the healer and deliverer of humanity on a spiritual and physical level. He has given me breath that I might live. Because I live and breathe I praise the One Who gave it all. Jesus again came to me and touched my mind and emotions. These emotions were awakened again in 2017.

In February, 2017, I received a text from Leslie that Joel had been diagnosed with brain cancer. What could be worse than this? I had lost my sister, my father, my son, and had the prospect of losing another son.

As a child, Joel was the one that would be the first to the front door to greet me when I returned home from work. He was the incredibly talented academic and musician. He was the driven one to succeed, with a work ethic second to none. He was the one passionate about reaching the fatherless, himself the father of seven children. I found myself demanding God to explain it, justify it…make sense of it all. Long buried feelings of grief and grieving surfaced again.

But God…is a Companion and Comforter. This is not an abstract feeling for me. Jesus' resurrection allows the Spirit of God to comfort my mind and emotions. And His comfort is faithful, even when I have my moments. I read once that there is no such thing as divine coincidences, but that those times are God-moments where He doesn't get the credit.

One such God-moment was who the receiving physician was in Vancouver, who coincidentally happens one of the most renowned brain surgeons on the west coast. God coincidentally provided Joel with a Jesus' name praying Christian oncologist. Joel has coincidentally survived nearly two years from the time of his initial diagnosis. These positive developments are God-moments. Because of Jesus Christ, God rewards those that continually look to Him. In Joel's case, God has granted length of days and a belief that all things work together for the good to those that love God and are the called according to His purposes.

In my case, God has given me peace of mind; I have hope for Joel's complete healing. If I should succumb to grief, then I have lost my hope. What this means is that there is something that assuages the grief. That something is only found in Jesus Christ.

The greatest struggle I have had has been my response to loss and grief. I am not a super believer. I do not have an extra portion of faith. I have not always been faithful, but I trust God. I am not waiting for God to do something. He already did, on the cross. Thankfully, I have a Savior, known to millions of others that have suffered grief and loss. He is known to Joel, and for that I am supremely thankful.

Jesus balances the playing field. He comforts those that grieve. He is the hope for mankind. On one glorious day in the future, God will deliver all who love and trust Him to a place of permanent life and peace. When the anniversary date of my younger son's death nears, I have normal moments of sadness. I choose not to stay there. It would be like camping in a graveyard. Jesus balances my grief with hope and peace. So what about the prospect of losing another son? By God's grace, I will trust. I will trust finished history in the cross and resurrection.

Part of Joel's treatment regimen is doing cross-fit exercises. God's balance to grief is my cross-grip; the hope and trust of the cross. While embracing Jesus, my hope and peace is secure. When grief crashes into your soul He is the only answer. Where else can anyone go but to Jesus? He is the hope of broken humanity. Hold on to Jesus; he heals and will heal the broken-hearted that trust in Him.

October 17, 2018
Devoted
S-Job 1:21; Acts 6:4
O-Job didn't blame God for his circumstance; and the work of leaders is prayer and the ministry of the Word!

_____
_____
_____

A-I'm not a victim of cancer. I must be devoted to prayer and the scripture!

_____
_____
_____

P-*Keep me from sinning against you in my circumstances! I will follow you!*

October 18, 2018
The Persecuted
S-Acts 9:5-6

O-Who is Jesus? The LORD! The church is the body of Jesus! When I am persecuted, Jesus is persecuted! Saul was confronted by Jesus and told what to do. Jesus calls everyone and those who listen and respond in faith have "marching orders." Jesus is the leader. Jesus is in command.

A-I must stop and ask Jesus what to do. He is in charge. I can be bold and confident knowing I will experience the persecution that Jesus did! Not just His own, or mine, but every believer! He is worthy and just.

P-*Jesus, remind me always to ask you what to do how to act* and *when/where to serve* and *share the gospel. You are LORD! Amen*

159

October 23, 2018
Noble Faith
S-Acts 17:11
O-The noble and better thing to do than blindly accept or contentiously argue is to search out truth in the Bible for yourself. The Bereans are solid examples to all believers. They did what every believer ought to do!

_____
_____
_____
_____
_____
_____

A-I need to search out the scripture for truth and not rely on others to teach me.

_____
_____
_____
_____
_____
_____

P-*Father, fill my heart with nobility to search your scripture for life and meaning!*

October 24, 2018
Trust God
S-Job 15:31; Acts 19:23-24
O-Trust in things or people is emptiness in the end. Money is empty as well. But so many people put their trust in it! And at the end, it can't save; it is empty. People who put money first will bring about conflict for people around them.

_____
_____
_____
_____
_____

A-There are times when I put my trust in medicine or supplements, or crossfit. Or even Leslie. But I must remember not to trust in money. MRI scans, supplements, crossfit or people. My trust must be in God thru Jesus. He is my healer and redeemer. He Himself is my peace, even as anxiety rises.

_____
_____
_____
_____
_____

P-*Lord, I'm anxious. About many things but mainly this twitching in my finger. Do I have another tumor fight coming? Prepare my heart. I fear no bad news. The LORD is my rock and my redeemer! Amen*

TIMEOUT - Provoked by Fatherlessness

Gabriel and Elijah Royce

When my sons were young, I took them to a Father and Son camp called, "Sons of Thunder." It takes place at Camp Tadmor. There is camping, fishing, kayaking, canoeing, swimming, paintball, .22 caliber rifle target shooting, obstacle courses, group challenges, walking stick whittling and carving, campfires and s'mores, eggs and bacon, hiking, high ropes course, archery, and many other things. It is an event for 1st-8th grade boys and their dads or fill in father figures.

The purpose is to teach lessons of manhood, from father to son. The camp sets you up as a dad for easy wins and provides some training for how to carry on the training back home. One year I even enlisted the help of a volunteer from the church to bring a fatherless boy.

Fatherlessness. It is a tragic, alarming, and growing epidemic in our culture. I remember serving as a youth pastor and studying the census data for my small town (Castle Rock, WA). I discovered that within my city's limits, with a population of about 2,000 people, there were at least 80 fatherless boys. It was unbelievable. I was provoked by this tragedy to do something about it. I tried to bring fatherless boys with me or through volunteers I could get to bring them to Camp Tadmor. We often had boys like these over to visit and/or spend the night. There were many conversations about being a man and taking responsibility that took place.

A few years ago, the last time I took my boys (and a fatherless boy with a volunteer mentor) there was a missionary with a display banner on the table by the auditorium; there I met Rob, a missionary representative for the ministry, "Fathers in the Field." It's a mentoring program whose vision is to "defend the cause of the fatherless…" This is a scripture from Isaiah that they use.

To defend the cause of the fatherless the ministry has 3 goals: faith (show the fatherless boy that there is a Heavenly Father who loves them), fatherhood (show the fatherless boy fatherly love and commitment), and forgiveness (show the fatherless boy the need to forgive their earthly father). Learn more at www.fathersinthefield.com

This was a perfect fit to my provocation. So I brought it to my city; it ended up being a collaboration between myself and the pastor of the St. Paul Lutheran church in Castle Rock. We identified a fatherless boy (aka "field buddy"), a "mentor father," and we paired them up. It's a three-year commitment for the mentor father and the field buddy. And it's incredibly effective in its' positive impact.

I called this Timeout "Provocation." The reason is because I believe God places passions in us in the areas of our gifting. When I saw the number of fatherless boys in my town, I was provoked to do something about it personally, by taking boys and mentoring them and by bringing a new ministry to my town.

Now, when you see some injustice or social issue in your community, and your talent, passion, or skillset pertains to that area, be provoked to take action.

Put faith to your feet and do something about the problem you're passionate about and do it for the glory of God!

October 25, 2018
Truth Reaction
S-Acts 22:22
O-Reactions to truth! Sometimes it doesn't go well. When you touch on people's sin, sometimes they will lash out in response.

_____
_____
_____
_____
_____
_____

A-I've learned over the years that even Christians will respond in anger when even gently confronted—from my dad, my wife and yours truly. Some people talk truth to you but not directly. It's behind your back. But I want to be like those who really follow the way. When I am confronted, I will respond without lashing out. And I'll gently confront rather than talk behind someone's back.

_____
_____
_____
_____
_____
_____

P-*Father. Let me receive correction with a gracious and humble spirit. I want to maintain self control at all times. Amen*

October 26, 2018
Answer the Bell
S-Acts 26:15-18

O-Paul was directly confronted by Jesus and given a purpose—to open the eyes of unbelievers—to turn them from darkness to light and from the power of Satan to God.

_____
_____
_____
_____
_____

A-When we get the answer to the question "Who are you Lord?" we must listen and respond in faith. Every believer in Jesus has a purpose to carry out. Whether to long life, untimely death, martyrdom, etc. Our purpose is to speak of what Jesus has done and of His forgiveness. Darkness: positive vibes and the Universe. Light: answered prayer and peace. Darkness: coincidences and karma. Light: God's sovereign plan and reaping what you sow. Darkness: fear, lies, and evil. Light: courage, truth, and good.

_____
_____
_____
_____
_____

P-*Jesus give me grace to answer the bell.* *Amen*

CHAPTER 5 – OVERTIME

October 30, 2018
Only Believe
S-Mark 5:29,36,41
O-The woman felt the healing in her body.
Later Jesus told her, your faith has made you well; go
in peace, and be healed of your disease. He had
already healed her—then said, go in peace and be
healed of your disease. Jesus reassured Jairus by
telling him not to fear but only believe. Jesus took
the little girl by the hand and said, "arise."

_____

_____

_____

_____

_____

_____

A-I remember the day I felt Jesus healing me in my brain. I felt heat in my tumor site that traveled down my neck. Oh, how I LONG to hear Jesus say to me, son, go in peace, and be healed of your disease! I'm comforted by Jesus' word to Jairus to not fear, but only believe. I wait for Jesus to say boy, arise. My future hope. Remember what God really said – "I won't take a husband. This doesn't end in death. You will have long life." I wish I never got sick, but then I wouldn't be here. "Don't fear, my son, only believe." This is so hard, yet simple. When I get symptoms or difficulty forming words or remembering things, I'll remember what God said thru others and trust Him. He is the same yesterday, today and tomorrow and forever. I will not fear, but only believe.

_____
_____
_____
_____
_____
_____

P-*Help me Lord. I believe but help me overcome my unbelief. I desire to serve you but even thru all this trial* and *suffering my flesh is still weak. Oh, God save me.*

October 31, 2018
Real Clean
S-Mark 7:21-23
O-Jesus declared all foods clean! He zeroed the problem with humanity down to 1 thing—the heart.

_____
_____
_____
_____
_____

A-What is the fruit in my life? Is it peaceable? Patient? Kind? I've been harsh with my children lately.

_____
_____
_____
_____
_____

P-*Father, I repent of my angry outbursts. Don't let my Keppra symptoms/side effects take over. Amen*

November 01, 2018
Shade
S-Psalms 121:5; Mark 10:36
O-The Lord is my keeper. He is my resting and peaceful place. He is shade from scorching heat. Jesus asks, what do you want me to do for you?

_____
_____
_____
_____
_____

A-I rest in the knowledge that God gives shade from scorching. I didn't get burns much in radiation. When the pressure is on He provides relief – like shade in a scorching sun. I feel He gave me radiation shade. I can just imagine how bold it was to request of Jesus – do whatever we ask. Bold as brass. But yet, I'm a son and don't boldly ask – so it will today – Jesus give me peace everyday and awareness of your healing in my life. I view MRIs as a part of this answer, but I seek a Word from you and not a doctor! So many have said to me, not this—he's going to make it. Then if this is you, speaking through them, will you send someone to say to may, go in peace, and be healed of your disease.

_____
_____
_____

P-*Heavenly father, thank you for shade. Amen.*

November 2, 2018
God of the Living
S-Mark 12:27

O-An amazing turn of phrase. God of the living, not of the dead. Not just turn of phrase but of power and authority. Words not just memorable, but weighty. Not only is there life after death in the resurrection, there is life after death before the resurrection! Abraham, Isaac and Jacob are deceased, but yet Jesus claims they are alive, frankly and boldly. To be absent from the body is to be present with the Lord.

_____
_____
_____
_____
_____

A-I'm comforted by Jesus' words—there is life after death and it is consciousness before the resurrection, in the presence of God—this is further evidenced by Moses and Elijah talking with Jesus during His transfiguration. I will hope and live in comfort in this regard. To live is Christ and to die is gain. Maranatha!

_____
_____

P-*Father, thank you for grace* and *forgiveness. Thank you for life after death. Let me be filled with boldness* and *courage to share my faith. Amen*

November 3, 2018
Faithful Friendship
S-Mark 14:33-34
O-Jesus trusted His friends. He relied on them to remain and watch. He was distressed and troubled in a way not recorded about Him before He shared what was going on inside with his trusted friends.

_____
_____
_____
_____
_____
_____
_____
_____

A-It is a wonderful thing to have friends you can trust to come with you and to share how you are really doing. It's a lesson in authenticity for sure. Am I open with others around me? Have I established close enough friendships with other men I can trust to share with? I have 3 men—Makana, Joe, and Trenton. Always Joe, but newly with Makana and Trenton. But it's also a lesson in love and patience. Jesus' friends let Him down by not watching or praying. He was in need. I need to be a faithful friend and I need to take a lesson from Jesus about when friends do let me down—when they don't follow thru. He still loved them.

_____
_____

_____

_____

_____

_____

_____

_____

_____

P-*Father, help me to be a faithful friend* and
to trust faithful friends. Amen

November 4, 2018
Already Dead
S-Mark 15:37,44
O-Jesus died on his own timing. It was a surprise to Pilate so much so that he sent the centurion to make sure Jesus had died.

_____
_____
_____
_____
_____

A-Jesus was in control of when he breathed His last. He did this work on the cross willingly and it amazes me, it astounds me that His love for me and the Father was displayed for all to see. "Truly, this was the son of God." Jesus' suffering was most holy and powerful. God's power is made perfect in weakness. The scene on the cross and the response of Pilate show this clearly.

_____
_____
_____
_____
_____

P-*Father, thank you for sending your son to die for my sins. Deliverance is made possible by the One who died already! Of His own accord. What power in Weakness. Teach me to suffer like Jesus. Amen*

November 5, 2018
Wisdom and Understanding
S-Job 28:28
O-It is wise to fear—respect, reverence God.
It is the application of wisdom or wisdom to turn
from evil—this is understanding.

_____
_____
_____
_____
_____

A-The wise and understanding work of man
is to fear God and turn to Jesus. The Christian life is
a daily choice to walk with Jesus. It's life in
marriage—choosing to love, relate, communicate and
move towards oneness.

_____
_____
_____
_____
_____

P-*Jesus, show me what my blind spots are*
and *give me grace* and *humility to accept discipline.*
Amen

CHAPTER 6 – POSTGAME - "the 7 Crowns in Heaven"

By Dale Royce and Joel Royce

The love and dedication and labor for the cause ended in a win. There are any number of teams and causes one can dedicate themselves to. How do you describe the greatest game of life? What analogies or metaphors can you use describing team wins?

Football is a great metaphor for team cohesion that leads to winning the game. The game of life is the same way. Teamwork and individual dedication are required to make life's endeavors a success. The lights are going down, the banged-up and bruised ballers are slowly gathering their personal items before one last huddle-up before leaving for home. Each one had fought hard, loved what they were doing, remained dedicated, earned respect and knew above everything else that they had left it all on the field of play. They had given until there was no more to give. The irony of it all is that although the season was now over, they wanted to play one more game.

There are accolades to be given for the Christian that lays it on the line; crowns to be given by the Lord himself. The goodness of God extends into eternity in unimaginable ways. When we get to Heaven, there are 7 crowns of reward: 1-righteousness, 2-victory, 3-imperishable, 4-life, 5-rejoicing, 6-glory, and 7-honor.

Crown of Righteousness

The first of these is for the one that finished well. They kept the faith through good times and the bad. This is a crown of righteousness. It is not a participation trophy. It is undeserved. But God himself provided it for those who answer His call. This crown comes with the words, 'Well done, good and faithful servant.'

"I have fought the good fight, I have finished the race, I have kept the faith. Henceforth there is laid up for me the crown of righteousness, which the Lord, the righteous judge, will award to me on that Day, and not only to me but also to all who have loved his appearing." (2 Timothy 4:7-8 ESV)

This is a promise, not just you but to all those who have longed for His appearing. There is a payback for finishing the race faithfully following Jesus. For how many people can say, I have kept the faith, and finished my race? Where the passage says "in store" it means laid up or kept in waiting. It's reserved in heaven with your name on it. It is more than a wreath—it's a crown of equity. We have the fulness of righteousness from Jesus; this is a crown of equal standing before God.

Crown of Victory

The second crown accolade to be given is a crown of victory. This crown is not stored in a trophy case to gather dust of a simple reminder of good memories. It is an ever-visible present reminder of the temperate self-discipline involved fighting the "good fight" of faith. It's worth noting that there aren't any short-cuts to living a godly life. This is the analogy Paul was using in 1 Corinthians 9. There are no short-cuts to strict training to win the games.

"Do you not know that in a race all the runners run, but only one receives the prize? So run that you may obtain it. Every athlete exercises self-control in all things. They do it to receive a perishable wreath, but we an imperishable. So I do not run aimlessly; I do not box as one beating the air. But I discipline my body and keep it under control, lest after preaching to others I myself should be disqualified." (1 Corinthians 9:24-27 ESV)

The 60 minutes in a game mirrors life itself; it passes by quickly. It is, in the light of eternity, less than a blip on a screen. The seeming impossible 4th and long to win with half a minute remaining seems almost impossible. Every ounce of precision and effort, long exercised, is now second nature. Instinctive response to what you have previously experienced makes you more than ready to be at the right place in the right time. Laying it on the line also means that achieving the win is doable. You want this win more than any single person or even yourself. You want it for everything the team represents. Implicit is the prospect of twisted ankles, broken bones, torn ligaments and tendons, unseen internal injuries and mental bruising, this being a contact sport. It involves having and using the tools you have learned to use and the courage to face whatever odds there are to win. The promise of a victor's crown is everlasting, not just a blip on the radar screen.

The crown of victory isn't for 'also-rans.' The work of the Gospel is not only for the pastor or the missionary. It is for the whole body of Christ. Every believer has at least one gift to serve the Lord with. You get a crown of victory if you run the race to win it with your gift(s). Do you work in construction? Work to the glory of God and reflect who He is when you bang your thumb between the nail and hammer, or when the customer doesn't pay you. Are you a finance manager? Work with integrity for the glory of God. Do you work from home? Are you a stay at home parent or a single parent? Apply yourself to be the best in all your roles, because in the end it is for God. You have a future and a hope for the victor's crown!

Imperishable Crown

In the days when Paul wrote his letter to the Corinthian church, he referenced Games and the strict training that the athletes adhered to. He observed that while they received a crown for winning, it was perishable. Literally. It was a crown made up of a wreath of leaves. They withered and dried out. Perished.

"Do you not know that in a race all the runners run, but only one receives the prize? So run that you may obtain it. Every athlete exercises self-control in all things. They do it to receive a perishable wreath, but we an imperishable. So I do not run aimlessly; I do not box as one beating the air. But I discipline my body and keep it under control, lest after preaching to others I myself should be disqualified." (1 Corinthians 9:24-27 ESV)

The crown that Paul is after is imperishable. A winner's crown that doesn't perish. And this is indicative and reflective of our eternal state! We too will be raised to life imperishable.

Crown of Life

This third crown is the crown of life. It is offered to those who stood firm, faithfully praying and trusting God during suffering, trials, and tribulations of many kinds.

"Do not fear what you are about to suffer. Behold, the devil is about to throw some of you into prison, that you may be tested, and for ten days you will have tribulation. Be faithful unto death, and I will give you the crown of life." (Revelation 2:10 ESV)

This crown is for those who experience suffering, trials, and tribulations, even to the point of their deaths. It's for the chronically ill person who refuses to give up faith in God's healing power. It's for the martyr who followed God's call to a violent tribe in some lost jungle. It's life-everlasting, as God intended it to be at the first.

Crown of Rejoicing

The ending game buzzer sounds with a rising cheer from the sidelines and the grandstands! The blood, sweat, tears experienced by the team ends with an unbelievable sense of joy and satisfaction of a job well-done. All the long hours of patiently teaching, training and mentoring has paid off with an impressive team win.

The end-game of this winning team was a combined effort that began with a call to play, learning to play each individual position well, accepting discipline and instruction and finally executing the plan for the team.

The teachers, mentors and coaches have no self-recriminations. They poured out their lives to the team and have unspeakable joy even while getting a Gatorade bath. The final buzzer will bring a crown of rejoicing! After the win is the party! And boy will there be a party in heaven.

"For what is our hope or joy or crown of boasting before our Lord Jesus at his coming? Is it not you? For you are our glory and joy. (1 Thessalonians 2:19-20 ESV).

"We will be caught up together with them in the clouds to meet the Lord in the air, and so we will always be with the Lord." (1 Thessalonians 4:17 ESV)

There will be such rejoicing! I think of the parable of the lost coin. There is so much joy for finding what was once lost, or like when I found my wallet I had lost three days earlier. However, this pales in comparison to the joy and rejoicing we'll participate in when we receive this crown! It is a rejoicing over injustices being righted; of every tear being wiped away; of every promise from God being fulfilled; of seeing God and finally being with Jesus in the flesh; and of being reunited with loved ones and dear friends.

Crown of Glory

Which teams do you think of when you en you hear the word "dynasty"? The 1960's UCLA basketball teams, the 1970's Pittsburgh Steelers, the 1990's-2000s NY Yankees? The current New England Patriots? These teams represented excellence in their play and were the standard-bearers of each respective sport. The common denominator in each of those franchises was their coaching strengths and skill levels of the players. Every successful team has a John Wooden, a Chuck Noll, a Joe Torre, or a Bill Billichek.

These coaches lived lives of excellence. They each did it for the love of the game. They emphasized the importance of integrity (well, the jury is out here on Bill!) and team unity. They demanded excellence in effort.

Pastors, coaches and mentors must understand that their insistence for team excellence was never in vain. Their crown of glory is a crown belonging to a dynasty; yet this crown fades and is forgotten; it is not eternal. The crown of glory for the believer, however, will never fade. It *is* eternal and it is prepared for the faithful follower of the way of Christ.

"So I exhort the elders among you, as a fellow elder and a witness of the sufferings of Christ, as well as a partaker in the glory that is going to be revealed: shepherd the flock of God that is among you, exercising oversight, not under compulsion, but willingly, as God would have you; not for shameful gain, but eagerly; not domineering over those in

your charge, but being examples to the flock. And
when the chief Shepherd appears, you will receive
the unfading crown of glory." (1 Peter 5:1-4 ESV)

For all the greatness of the teams just
mentioned, again, those memories fade; those
trophies collect dust. Eventually, time dims the
record of the dynasty and people have no immediate
feeling of respect for the accomplishments of the
past.

When we get to Heaven, you will receive the
crown of glory, which never fades! It will last, not
for centuries, or even a millennia; it lasts for eternity
which stands outside of time.

Crown of Honor

Something that brings or is worthy of honor is honorable. This crown is honorable because the teams' owner insisted in principled, honest and ethical behavior. Serving was never beneath them. They never insisted upon doing anything that they would not have done themselves. Every coach, player, pastor and saint must have a stake in the vision and sacrifice of the owner.

"But we see him who for a little while was made lower than the angels, namely Jesus, crowned with glory and honor because of the suffering of death, so that by the grace of God he might taste death for everyone." (Hebrews 2:9 ESV)

The game is finally over. The precious mentors have literally given their lives as living sacrifices in order to see their team succeed. Each of the victor's crowns is fully earned. They have fought the good fight. They have kept the faith.

The most powerful crown these victors possess are embraced securely in the arms of God. Their pure crowns ride with the owner. The crowns on the head of the owner are those that held dear his gospel message of hope. The many crowns on our returning Lord is an ownership crown, the claim of the mighty God himself staking permanent claim on those whom he called, were chosen and faithful.

"And I heard a loud voice in heaven, saying, "Now the salvation and the power and the kingdom of our God and the authority of his Christ have come, for the accuser of our brothers has been thrown down, who accuses them day and night

before our God. 11 And they have conquered him by the blood of the Lamb and by the word of their testimony, for they loved not their lives even unto death." (Revelation 12:10-11 ESV)

"His eyes are like a flame of fire, and on his head are many diadems, and he has a name written that no one knows but himself. He is clothed in a robe dipped in blood, and the name by which he is called is The Word of God." (Revelation 19:12-13 ESV)

The crown of honor will be dazzling, however, it will utterly pale before the beauty, glory and majesty of the Lord Jesus Christ.

CHAPTER 7   LINKS to Photos and
Game Films

(For hyperlinks and more photos visit
www.calvaryhillpublishing.com)

Photo credit Brian Drake

Joel Royce, #54 for the Cowlitz Cobras

http://tdn.com/sports/cowlitz-county-cobras-laying-
the-groundwork/article_11955d12-042d-5bf8-a875-
61ae990a6752.htm

Some of Joel's football game video highlights

https://www.hudl.com/profile/7205809/Joel-Royce?fbclid=IwAR0VZQzoogVgbjlb1m6cM--qybFL8legy-cF57M04FOYHfAG1PLHKThm8Fw

Cobras in playoff game YouTube
https://www.youtube.com/watch?v=6optt55oRdUb
See Joel at the 35 minute mark, then watch the prayer after game with BOTH TEAMS!

Another Cobras game
https://www.youtube.com/watch?v=e5gTN9XW5QM

Lions Club Rotary Club Presentation of Cobras by Joel
http:/wwww.youtube.com/watch?v=PYwLEvWqDWg
"My vision to have something BIGGER than football to address some of the problems in our community" alcoholism, drug use, fatherlessness, young men to learn self-control/discipline/anger management
"it's not just about playing a game, it's about being a part of the community"

(For hyperlinks and more photos visit
www.calvaryhillpublishing.com)

194

Agape Photography by Reveena

(For hyperlinks and more photos visit
www.calvaryhillpublishing.com)

Appendix A
Scripture Index

1 Corinthians 9:24	59
1 Corinthians 9:25	62
1 Corinthians 9:26	64
1 Corinthians 9:27	66
1 Corinthians 15	1
1 Thessalonians 4:13-14	74
2 Chronicles 33:16	98
Acts 17:11	157
Acts 19:23-24	158
Acts 22:22	162
Acts 26:15-18	163
Acts 3:15	147
Acts 4:11,14	148
Acts 6:4	155
Acts 9:5-6	156
Daniel 6:26b-27	125
Ephesians 6:10	33
Ephesians 6:16	34
Ezekiel 33:11	119
Ezekiel 37:4	29
Ezekiel 45:10	122

Galatians 6:1	19
Haggai 2:4c	137
Isaiah 26:4	27
Isaiah 64:4a	96
Isaiah 65:24	97
Jeremiah 1:7-8,17	104
Jeremiah 5:20-21	107
Job 1:21	155
Job 15:31	158
Job 28:28	172
John 1:48-49	95
John 11:3-4,32b-33,51	105
John 12:19,27,42	107
John 13:8b,10,34-35,44a,50	112
John 3:33-36	97
John 6:5,29,44	100
John 7:37-39	101
John 8:24,28,31,34-36	102
John 9:37	103
Lamentations 3:21	15
Lamentations 3:22-26	116
Luke 1:15b,45	122
Luke 10:16,20,22	137
Luke 11:13,23	138
Luke 12:3	139
Luke 13:11-13	140

Luke 16:10-11	143
Luke 2:29-32	123
Luke 4:13	126
Luke 5:16	127
Luke 6:42d	128
Luke 7:50	131
Luke 8:46,48	132
Malachi 3:18	149
Mark 10:36	191
Mark 12:27	168
Mark 14:33-34	169
Mark 15:37,44	171
Mark 5:29,36,41	164
Mark 7:21-23	166
Matthew 11:28-30	67
Matthew 24:12	49
Micah 4:2	42
Nahum 1:7	99
Nehemiah 1:5	145
Nehemiah 4:4	146
Philippians 4:19	40
Proverbs 1:26-27	85
Proverbs 18:1	47
Proverbs 19:20	17
Proverbs 19:20-21	13
Psalm 103:11	93

Psalm 30:5	44
Psalm 86:11	51
Psalms 1:3	147
Psalms 121:5	191
Psalms 126:1-3	141
Psalms 127:3-4	133
Psalms 131:2	144
Psalms 133:1	145
Psalms 138:7	143
Psalms 147:10-11	142
Psalms 48:13-14	114
Psalms 84:11	131
Revelation 12:10	113
Revelation 13:10	114
Revelation 14:7,12-13	115
Revelation 16:7	117
Revelation 17:14	118
Revelation 19:6-9,10d	120
Revelation 22:6-7	121
Romans 14:12	87
Romans 14:8-9	53
Romans 15:13	55
Song of Solomon 2:13	57
Zechariah 4:6	139
Zephaniah 3:17a	103

Appendix B Topic Index

Already Dead	171
Answer the Bell	163
Arrows	133
Bear Witness	102
Builders	148
By The Spirit	139
Can't Fool God	66
Can't Hide from God	87
Desolate Prayer	127
Devoted	155
Distinction	149
Do the Deeds	120
Done Great Things	141
Don't be Afraid to Ask	17
Don't Isolate Yourself	47
Dwell in Unity	145
Faith for Healing (Stable MRI News!)	132
Faith Shield	34
Faithful Friendship	169
Fear and Glorify God	115
Finding Strength	33
Forget Happiness?	15
Frontlines	64
Get to Work	137
Go in Peace (MRI Day)	131
God Hears	97
God is True	117
God Meets Needs	40

God Never Fails	116
God of Action	96
God of Hope	55
God of the Living	168
God Sends and Delivers	104
God's Pleasure	119
God's Promise	142
God's Ways	42
Grief	74
Head on a Swivel!	19
Heart	51
Heart Water	101
Holy Spirit: The Greatest Gift	138
How, God?	122
I Saw You	95
Joy and Peace	44
Lamb Chops!	118
Listen to Advice	13
Lord of the Living Dead	53
Mr Log-Eye	128
Next Gen	114
Noble Faith	157
Offer Sacrifices	98
Only Believe	164
Operation: Enduring Kingdom	125
Painted Rocks	27
Preservation	143
Quieted by Love	103
Real Clean	166
Respect the Game	49
Ripe on the Vine	57

Run the Race	59
Salvation Has Come	113
Shade	191
Simeon Speaks	123
Steadfast Love	93
Success	62
Take Refuge	99
Taunt Turns	146
Temptation Comes	126
The Author	147
The Bread Test	100
The Persecuted	156
The Resurrection	105
The Weaned	144
Trust God	158
Trustworthy and True	121
Truth Reaction	162
Unlooked for Healing	140
Washed by Jesus	112
God's Weigh Station	67
When the End Comes	107
Wisdom and Understanding	172
Open to Wisdom	85
Words of Life!	29

Not the end

Made in the USA
Monee, IL
01 February 2020